FROM TRAGEDIES

to Happiness

MY TRUE STORIES

LORI M. RADOSNY

authorHOUSE®

AuthorHouse™
1663 Liberty Drive
Bloomington, IN 47403
www.authorhouse.com
Phone: 1 (800) 839-8640

Published by AuthorHouse 03/25/2015

ISBN: 978-1-4969-7250-7 (sc)
ISBN: 978-1-4969-7249-1 (e)

Print information available on the last page.

Contents

INTRODUCTION

My name is Lori Radosny and I have written this book to share with you some of the good things about the transcription profession. I also have written about my personal life and the things that have happened to me in the past.

My brother, Walt, was a court reporter who died in 2006 and he always said that he would write a book about his experiences and funny things that happened in court. I think he is up in heaven giving me the inspiration to write this book.

I wrote the 2-line rhymes in three days. They just kept coming to me one after another so I want to share them with you. Also, there are some songs that I came up with regarding the transcription profession that I hope you enjoy.

My personal life has had some bumps and bruises along the way but as my good friend, Jessie, always says, "Keep hope alive."

I want to thank Dave Herzig. Honey, you are my rock and I wouldn't have made it long without you. Thank you for all you do for me. I truly appreciate it.

I am not a mental health professional so please see someone if you need to do so. I am just sharing my experiences of my tragedies.

I hope with this book to convey one message. If you go through 1 tragedy or 10, they do not define you as a person. You can take care of your tragedies the best you can and always move forward. Always look to the future and you will be happy. You can never totally forget your tragedies because they did happen to you and are a part of you. But put them on the back burner so to speak. While some tragedies may take longer to work through, you can be sure that happiness will come your way.

In the book I say Rad for radiologist and MT for medical transcriptionist.

Love,
Lori

Chapter 1

To my Sweetheart, Dave Herzig,

Before I start telling my life story, I want to share a love story with you.

It's called, Because You Waited.

At the hospital, they said "go out and meet people, find an activity." I never bowled a day in my life but I decided to join a Friday Night Bowling League at the local bowling alley. A summer league. I believe that my mom who died two years earlier of lung cancer sent me there to meet you. She knew that you would take care of me.

I walked in the door of the bowling alley not knowing anybody, seeing new faces and surroundings. It was there I saw you for the first time. I knew immediately that you were different in a good way. Kind and funny. Every week after that I couldn't wait until Friday so we could see each other and talk and have fun. I then had to wait another week. We had a good group in our league. I was laughing more than I was bowling. After we were done bowling we would all go into the bar and have a few drinks and talk and laugh. I remember when our teams played each other the first time. I was so excited. You had me by the second frame of the first game. I knew that I wanted to spend the rest of my life with you. But I was scared a little. I never had a man in my life. I was too fearful because of what the man in the garage did to me when I was about 9 years old. But the more I got to know you, the more I trusted you.

One time when we were in the bar after bowling, a man asked me to dance. He asked you if he could and you said to him go for it. But I wouldn't do it. I can't dance with any man except my Boo.

I know that you had a bad breakup with your ex. You were hurt and pissed off. I wanted to let you know that the day of that breakup was the luckiest day of my life because I then got to meet you.

The song that most reminds me of you is "The First Time Ever I Saw Your Face" by Roberta Flack. The first time ever I saw your face, kissed your mouth, lay with you. Listen to that song's words very closely and you will see why. Part of the lyrics I have here:

"The first time ever I lay with you,
I felt your heart so close to mine and
I knew our joy would fill the earth
and it would last til the end of time, my love."

Another song I came across recently is "At Last" by Etta James. Look at those lyrics and listen to the song and that is you. A part of it is here:

"A dream I can call my own
I found a thrill, to press my cheek to
A thrill that I have never known."

We went out on our first official date on September 3, 1989. It was special to me in many, many ways. First it was my birthday but you didn't know that until we said goodnight. We went out to dinner and then saw When Harry Met Sally and we had to sit in the front row with our heads bent back so we could see the movie screen. It was there that you held my hand for the first time. I have had many firsts with you. First man to go on a date with, first phone call with a guy, first movie, first man to hold my hand, first kiss, first (free) dinner, first everything if you know what I mean.

I made you wait until February 17, 1990 for our first romantic session. I made you wait 167 days until that day. I think that deepened our relationship because we got to know each other so well in that time. Any other man would probably have walked away. But you waited. I was still scared to do anything but you were very gentle and kind. I was still living at home and so were you. Then your parents went on vacation for a week. And that special day happened. It will always be a special day for me. I don't remember exactly when I told you about the molestation but I think it was pretty far into our relationship so you

2

didn't understand why I waited so long. They say a woman wants a man like her dad. I found that in you. You were kind, considerate and funny.

We have been together now for 25 years. It seems like only yesterday that I met you. It couldn't be 25 whole years. But it is.

I know that because of your bad breakup prior to me that you are fearful that I will cheat on you or leave you. Honey, I would never do those things to you. We have been through too much together. Family member deaths, hospitalizations, emergency room visits, money issues, paying the bills, death of our dog, and all the day-to-day things that come up. I know that I say that guy is cute, that other guy is handsome, or that other guy is hot. I only look, I would never do anything to jeopardize our relationship because you waited. I couldn't do that to you. You are my Boo.

After I hit my head on a door in 2011, I knew that you worried about me because I could see the concern in your face. You were scared that when I drove you down to the bus stop every day that I might not find my way home. I had concussion symptoms for about 2-1/2 years after that accident and things were very fuzzy to me. I really don't recall those years.

Even though all the issues we go through, I would live with you in a tent under a bridge along with our dog, Sullivan. As long as I was with you, nothing else matters. We would be happy. All three of us.

If a man knocked on the door and came in, got on one knee and said Lori I have this 30 carat diamond ring for you. You are the most beautiful woman I have ever seen. I am worth 100 zillion dollars, you will never have to work a day in your life or worry about money ever again. Will you marry me? I would ask him can you quote lines from Seinfeld, Big Bang Theory, Larry, Moe, Curly or the Flintstones? He would say no. I would say take a hike buddy. I'm staying with my Dave.

I think what is so neat is that during all the years together we have had something to laugh about. Whether it's lines from a TV show, movie, our family members, whatever comes up.

You don't think that you take care of me and Sullivan that great. You take care of us every day. More than you know. You take Sullivan for walks, clean up his poop, come home tired from work but you still make me dinner. You also wash my clothes and clean the house. You call us at 10 a.m., 12 noon, and 2 p.m. every day while you are at work. You worry if I don't answer on the first ring. You think I might have fallen down the steps or left you. Leaving you would never happen. I want you to realize that.

I remember when I first started listening to the radio regularly. American Authors came out with a song called The Best Day Of My Life and I made you listen to it. Then I saw Ricky Martin's video and song called The Best Thing About Me Is You. Those two songs changed my life forever. If you listen to the words in both songs, especially Ricky's, you know why. In Ricky's song there are lines that say:

Life is short so make it what you wanna, make it good, don't wait until manana, I think I'm cool cause your name's on this heart shaped tattoo. Now the best thing about me is you.

These are words to live by and I try to every day. You know about the tattoo and my reason for getting it. I also have told you more than once about something I read in a book. It was about a 100-year-old woman. She only had two pieces of cheese and a small tomato in her refrigerator, but she felt blessed every day. Think about that a minute. I feel blessed every day that I met you. I always asked the Lord for a man to make me happy and make me laugh. It took 28 years but he did come through. I met you.

I don't care that much about material things any more. Sure, I've had $800 purses and wallets, more books that haven't even been read yet, so many DVD's and CD's that haven't been opened yet, more jewelry than

I can wear, more perfume, so much workout equipment that I haven't even used. Those things don't matter to me any more. I have you and Sullivan and that's what is important to me now.

During my third hospitalization for depression I made a plaque made of ceramic that has white flowers on it and I put it in a wooden frame. When things get really tough I look at it and say to myself that there is nothing that can happen where I would ever want to attempt suicide again. I haven't looked at that plaque in a long time because I now have you. You have saved my life so many times, more than you know. We are a match made in heaven. You keep my head out of the oven and I keep your head out of the oven, practically on a daily basis. I seriously think that if I hadn't met you in 1989 that I would have attempted suicide again and would have succeeded. Thank you for saving my life, honey.

We have many happy memories and some sad. But mostly happy. I wrote this book to share with people my tragedies that happened in hopes that I can help someone. My biggest tragedy was my brother Walt's death. That was the hardest one to face. But you helped me through it. You were there every day while I cried thinking of my brother, holding me and saying everything would be okay.

I recently watched an America's Got Talent video. On it was a 20-year-old woman named Anna. At the age of 16 she was diagnosed with anxiety-depressive disorder. She said before she came out on stage that she didn't want to be here anymore and she didn't know how to bring herself out of her depression. That is exactly how I felt when I was severely depressed. Then she found music. She auditioned for the show in front of Howie Mandell and Howard Stern and two woman who I don't know. She came on stage and Howie asked her name. She said Anna. He asked what she did for a living. She said she didn't have a job because of her situation. Howie asked what was her situation. She explained and Howie said to her that he also has an anxiety disorder, he has OCD, and people don't understand what we go through. She then sang the song Hallelujah. Very beautifully. Howie got up from his seat when she finished and walked up on stage. He then gave her a big hug which he normally doesn't do to people because of his own issues. I believe that we see things and hear things to teach us lessons. I was meant to see that video. It has been 44 years since my molestation. I feel that if Anna could get up on that stage and sing in front of hundreds of people that I can now lose weight successfully. I think I kept my weight on as a safety net, that way no one would ever molest me again or possibly rape me. I don't have that fear anymore after seeing Anna's story. I don't use food anymore as a safety mechanism. I will lose the weight to be beautiful for you and Sullivan. Even when I was at my heaviest which was about 260 pounds, you still thought I was beautiful. And I love you for that.

I have only one regret in our relationship. That I couldn't give you a baby. It would be a boy. And we would name him Roy Honus Herzig. To honor the two most important men in your life, your father and grandfather. And you could play catch with him and watch him play in little league baseball. I talked with my gynecologist because I thought that the molestation "scared" me into not going through puberty. He said it was probably a genetic reason and not the molestation.

If someone were to ask me to write the most beautiful love story in the world, I would taken pen to paper and rewrite word for word the story I just told you. I feel we have the most beautiful love story ever told. I will love you forever in my heart because you saw something I didn't see in myself, beauty inside and out. As Ricky Martin says, the best thing about me is you. I will update our love story 25 years from today's date (October 20, 2014). That will be in the year 2039. We will be 78 years old. If I may, I would like to quote one more song that is you in seven simple words. It is Barry White's song You're the First, The Last, My Everything. I will write in the year 2039 that our love has deepened each year more and more for the past 50 years. We will love each other until our dying breath. I will always love you, because you waited.

Love, Lori

The Professional Part:

Chapter 2

HISTORY OF MEDICAL TRANSCRIPTION:

Medical Transcription is a method of typing out a patient's medical record whether it involves a hospital visit, doctor's office visit or Radiology report. It has been around since doctors started treating patients.

Doctors used to do document all the information and it was turned over to medical stenographers in the early 1900's. Items used to document the information started with typewriters, electronic typewriters, word processors and now computers. Tape recorders were first used in the middle 1900's.

Now the doctor's offices are using the electronic health record to document patient information. The Medical Transcriptionist, in my opinion, is becoming a dying breed because the physicians put in the information on patients by themselves and do not need transcriptionists as much as before.

Chapter 3

I RESPECT RADIOLOGISTS:

Unlike specialists who concentrate on certain body parts, and in their fields who are very skilled, the radiologists have to know everything about the body including:

Musculoskeletal system, nervous system, arteriovenous system, cardiovascular system, lymphatic system, the senses, endocrine system, circulatory system, respiratory system, digestive system, genitourinary system, obstetrics, gynecology, and the reproductive system. They have to know the whole shebang!

They find blood clots, fractures, strokes, baby problems in the womb, foreign bodies and dislocations. This isn't a complete list. They have to know all the abnormalities, diseases, disorders, syndromes, cancers, and congenital anomalies that happen in the body. Imagine if we didn't have them today. It would be like the old Gunsmoke days with Doc not being able to find what is wrong with the patient.

I feel that radiologists are the 'unseen' heroes in the health care setting. Patients don't usually see them in the facilities but the radiologist provides valuable information to the patient and their physician who is treating them.

Chapter 4

2-LINE RHYMES – PART 1

Everyday MT's use their phalanges and craniums,
but we know we'd rather be out planting geraniums.

We can't forget the dedication of pathology MT's and the wonderful jobs they perform,
they provide vital information and never misinform.

The acute care transcriptionists painstakingly type reports to their greatest ability,
so they can send the urgent information needed at the facility.

I type hard words everyday like oblique and transverse,
so surely I deserve that new designer purse.

Let us not forget the men who work with us as a team,
but I am certain as they type those medical terms they too sometimes scream.

In 1985 we were praised for the work we do,
if you ask me, it was long overdue.

I must finish this report before the end of my shift,
but I'll be very careful because I have a great gift.

Not another addendum, I've had my fill,
couldn't they just describe an eosinophil.

Who invented auto corrects deserves a great big hug,
without them I would my computer unplug.

Lori M. Radosny

In my queue I see a STAT,
don't worry, this MT will take care of that.

I must take a short break if you please,
I have to stretch my arthritic hands and knees.

I thought the doctor said the patient was in traction,
but really he was talking about an ejection fraction.

Don't fret, I'm writing these sentences as I go,
sometimes it gets tough to rhyme all the time you know?

I may not know the meaning of all the words I hear,
But I can kick butt spelling them and a word book is very near.

When people talk loud in the background while the doc dictates,
don't they realize there is a transcriptionist getting irate?

My favorite impression is "no acute abnormality,"
as that is good news to the PCP and patient's mentality.

Where would health care be without Radiology and the technology today,
It's important to know the radiologists are reading films for us every day.

I've once or twice seen some images of a CT, MRI and ultrasound,
those talented radiologists perform tasks that are superbly profound.

We can't leave out Support, they can fix my computer, I give them no guff,
they had to go to school to learn all this technical stuff.

If I can't hear a word I say loudly "WHAT?"
Dave's sleeping in the next room, I better keep my mouth shut.

As I turn my computer off at the end of my day,

I say to myself I'm happy I got to transcribe today.

I like to look quickly at patient's age and DOB (date of birth),
isn't that beautiful, I once saw the patient is 103.

I also like looking at the patient's names and see the creativity,
I better get back and work on my productivity.

Whomever invented auto correct deserves a big pat on the back,
without it I would be typing so much extra like a total maniac.

I hit my head on a door in 2011, this is a true story,
CT came back normal but it was a concussion for little old Lori.

As I leave you now, I must relate,
All these rhymes I can no longer tolerate.

One more thing before I exit,
all transcriptionists remember you are all exquisite.

I start at work at 4 and be dutiful,
but now I have to watch The Bold and The Beautiful.

I'm done with my work, I need a good rest,
but first I have to tidy my desk.

In auto corrects I have long words and phrases you see,
for spondylolisthesis I use the letters SPE.

Obstetric ultrasounds I think are my favorite I yell,
I love to hear that mom and baby are doing well.

The term reboot is always a funny word to me,
while my computer boots up I grab a green tea.

What exactly is the pineal gland?
I'm pretty sure it's not located in your left or right hand.

Ladies out there, don't forget to get your mammogram performed.
Let's just hope the technologist's hands are lukewarm.

I just transcribed a two view pelvis,
Do you think the patient could be Elvis?

I transcribed the report, it looked splendid,
OMG I forgot to send it.

It's called the humerus, must be how it is spelled,
A fracture in this area is not comical I yelled.

Last year I had a CT scan for some constipation,
Got a copy of the report because I had to snoop,
Not anywhere on there did it mention any poop.

I could type 50 chest x-rays all in a row and never complain,
I'm not sure why, it's hard to explain.

History reads: 53-year-old with tiredness, confusion, hair turning gray,
Hey, that sounds like me on any given day.

I came to visit you but soon I'll see ya,
I hear you nave nausea, vomiting and diarrhea.

Chapter 5

TRANSCRIPTION SONGS

These are songs I made up from the original songs and I have included the singer who sang the original song. You can play a game with others by saying my transcription song title and see if they can name the artist who sang the original.

(Transcriptionist screaming with Joy) Another Day in Paradise – Phil Collins

My Sweet Lord (help me to hear this word) – George Harrison

Transcriptionist to Rad. You Are Mumbling a Little (Please) Do It Again – The Beach Boys

Sometimes I Type Faster on Friday – Britney Spears

I Wanna Be a Great Transcriptionist – Spice Girls

Transcriptionist to Rad – Take My Breath Away – Berlin

Rads Don't Lie – Shakira & Wyclef Jean

Please Don't Interrupt Me, I don't Want To Miss The Next Word – Aerosmith

All You Need Is a Good CT Scan Of The Head Report – The Beatles

When Transcriptionists Cry It's Usually A Difficult Word To Make Out – Prince

My Favorite Rad Is Dictating, It Will Be A Great Day After All – U2

A Hard Day of Dictating – The Beatles

I Transcribe Fine – The Beatles

I Got Transcription Fever – Bee Gees

What's Medical Terminology Got To Do With It? - Tina Turner

Why Can't You Read This? M.C. Hammer

Bad Dictator – Lady Gaga

Have you Ever Met A Rad? Bryan Adams

Don't Stop Dictating Now, It's only 10 a.m. – Fleetwood Mac

I Still Haven't Found The Spelling Of That Artery I'm Looking For – U2

I Heard It Through The Voice Player – Marvin Gaye

Your Dictation Means So Much More Than Just A Line Count – Extreme

I Want To Know What Body Habitus Means – Foreigner

I Hope You Dictate Until The End Of My Shift – Perry Como

I Can Hear Clearly Now the Static Is Gone – Johnny Nash

These Are The Best Of My Anatomy – The Emotions

Radiologists Just Want To Have a Coffee Break – Cyndi Lauper

Never Can Say Anything Bad About My Reports – Gloria Gayner

I Feel A Lot of Love When the Rads Say Please and Thank You – Donna Summer

Men In The Reading Room – Will Smith

Do You Really Want Me To Transcribe This – Culture Club

Crazy For Your Ultrasound Reports – Madonna

The Most Talented MT In The World – Prince

Listen To Your Own Dictating – Roxette

You Were Meant To Read An X-Ray For Me – Jewell

Rolling In The X-Ray Reports – Adele

Please Don't Pause Now, I'm Here Waiting – Richard Marx

You Can't Hurry Transcription – Phil Collins

Her Transcription Drive Me Crazy – Fine Young Cannibals

Dictated With A Kiss – Brian Hyland

Rad to MT – I Dictate This Way – Run DMC and Aerosmith

A Good Dictating Rhythm Is The Answer – Snap

Rad to MT – You Ain't Heard Nothing Yet – Bachman-Turner Overdrive

What Did I Just Transcribe? – Ray Charles

When You Retire, I'll Be so Glum – Mariah Carey & Whitney Houston

Crying in the Reading Room – Elvis Presley

No Other MD Compares to You – Sinead O'Connor

But transcriptionist don't cry….sometimes we really do – Fergie

Hey Rad Take a Bow – Madonna

We Cherish Our Rads – Kool And The Gang

Don't Be Cruel To Your MT – Elvis Presley

A Transcriptionist's Plea, Help – The Beatles.

I Want To Do Your Dictations – The Beatles

Don't Stop The Dictations – Rihanna

Endless Dictations – Diana Ross & Lionel Richie

I Can't Make Out A Word and I'm All By Myself – Celine Dion

Please Shout A Little Louder – Tears For Fears

Every Dictation You Make – The Police

I've Been Transcribing practically All Of My Life – K-Ci and JoJo

SOS, I Can't Make Out This Word – Abba

Finally the End Of The Dictation – Boyz II Men

Without Me, Who Would Do Your Reports – Eminem

I Didn't Get That Phrase, Baby One More Time – Brittney Spears

You're The One That I Want To Dictate – John Travolta & Olivia-Newton John

I Will Survive This 10 Minute Long Report – Gloria Gaynor

Speak Louder, I'm Getting A Careless Whisper – George Michael

Don't Speak Now, I'm Going To Lunch – No Doubt

How Deep Is Your Voice – Bee Gees

Jive Dictatin' – Bee Gees

More Than A Transcriptionist – Bee Gees

I've Got To Get an Email To You – Bee Gees

How Can You Mend A Broken Dictating Machine – Bee Gees

No More Tears (Enough Is Enough) Of That Dictating – Donna Sommer

She Transcribes Hard For The Money – Donna Sommer

Hard Headed Transcriptionists – Elvis

Are You Dictating Tonight? – Elvis

Suspicious Transcriptionist – Elvis

How Can You Mend A Broken Microphone – Bee Gees

Transcribing Queen – Abba

If I Can't Have Your Reports – Yvonne Elliman

Man! I Feel Like A Talented Transcriptionist – Shania Twain

Your Dictations Don't Impress Me Much – Shania Twain

You Give Good Paragraphs – Whitney Houston

All The Rad I Need – Whitney Houston

I Want To Transcribe For Somebody Who Appreciates My Work – Whitney Houston

Point Of No Return In The Dictation – Expose

As Long As I Can Transcribe – Expose

I Wish You Were Done Dictating – REO Speedwagon

Hot Vocal Cords – Rod Stewart

The First Dictation In The Morning Is The Deepest – Rod Stewart

Could I Have This CT Scan Report – Anne Murray

Don't It Make You Want To Dictate? Bonnie Raitt

Look What You've Done To My Beautiful Report – Boz Scaggs

Here Comes The Radiologist to Dictate Some More Ultrasounds – Mickey Gilley

Dictator Pleasures – Barbra Steisand

Chapter 6

TYPE-RIGHT TRANSCRIPTION SERVICE, OWNER, LORI RADOSNY

I decided to start my own transcription service while still working full time.

I got work from a Cardiology office and I knew I couldn't do it all on my own. I put an ad in the paper and looked for a part-time transcriptionist to help me. At this point I decided to go part time at the doctor's office because I wanted to get more work for my one-woman company. Make it big. Well it didn't happen.

I looked for transcription jobs in my area but there was nothing available. I was looking online and found a position for a Radiology (my first love) medical transcriptionist. You could work at home and do the transcribing there. I looked into it, applied and got the job thankfully. I had to learn a lot because I didn't know anything about remote typing.

I have given up on Type-Right Transcription Service for now. The doctor's offices aren't hiring transcriptionists because they are all getting electronic medical records and putting all the information in themselves. My doctor's office I go to told me it is some kind of law now. Either the doctor does that or does voice recognition dictating. They talk into a recorder on the computer and his/her words come up in the report on the screen. Technology is getting scary. It can do so much now. In the old days of transcription the doctor used a dictator and dictated on mini cassettes and then the transcriptionist would type from them. They were kind of a pain because the tape would sometimes bunch up in the player or would tear.

Chapter 7

TO THE BEST RADIOLOGIST IN THE WORLD.....NO KIDDING!

There are doctors I type for who are very good at dictating. They do a wonderful job. But there is one doctor I type for at my job. He is the best. He gives you the patient's name, medical record number, name of the study, date the study was done, any comparisons or techniques used, and then dictates a perfect report. He never drifts from this dictating format. I could probably count on my first 2 fingers how many times I had a blank in his reports since I started there in 2008. He has a wonderful strong voice and dictates at a pace that I rarely have to take my foot off the pedal and repeat what he said. If he stumbles on a word which is like almost never he will stop for a second, back up and say what he wanted to say.

If I see his name under the dictation section on my screen I immediately am in a great mood and look forward to doing his reports. I say it's going to be a great day after all. And it is! Since he does the same format every time you get in what I call a typing rhythm and can go faster than with other dictators. If my boss called me and said this doctor just dictated 100+ reports, can you help out, I would say I will do them all! It might take me a day and a half but I would happily do it for him. He could dictate the phone book and I would be just as happy. Someday I'm going to contact the transcription association to see if there is some sort of Golden Vocal Cord Award he could receive. Doctor, you are truly appreciated. Thank you.

Chapter 8

YOU WERE BORN WHEN?

I always look at the patient's birthday and age when I transcribe. I think it is so cute when I see a patient with one of the birthdays below.

New Year's Day

Valentine's Day – You would be amazed at the number of people with this one.

Fourth of July

Halloween

Christmas Eve

Christmas

New Year's Eve

Some patients come into the hospital even on their birthday.

Chapter 9

PROS AND CONS OF WORKING AT HOME: (These assume you are the only one at home.)

PROS:

- Can wear your bikini to work if you want. You can also wear your pajamas and slippers to work. Do those two things in a regular office and they are calling for someone to come get you.
- Doesn't matter if the clothes are clean and/or they are ironed. It's okay I gave them the quick sniff test.
- Can swear loudly and no one hears. Make sure the windows are closed.
- If it's snowing outside I laugh loudly. I am already at work and don't have to drive anywhere.
- Can crack your gum and not annoy anybody.
- Let noises come out of every orifice (hole) on your body. Who cares?
- Can go to the movies during the day when it's not crowded.
- Can go leisurely go shopping during the day when it's also not crowded.
- Can apologize to your dog or cat for bumping them in the nose and no one thinks that is weird.
- You can bond with your pet more.
- You can decorate your home office any way you want.
- Don't have to put your pooch in doggy day care. Save money.
- Can feed your pet at 2:00 p.m. when he/she is really hungry instead of waiting until 6:00 p.m. when you get home.
- If working late shift, can make day appointments for doctor's office, to go for a mammogram, other x-ray or bloodwork at the hospital.
- Can take a nap before work and be refreshed.

- Can have a variety of foods from the refrigerator for lunch instead of the same old baloney sandwich or that salad that is wilted by the time you eat it.
- Save money on a babysitter Monday through Friday.
- Can throw something in the slow cooker or oven and it can be ready in time for dinner rather than making everything when you get home from work.
- If your pet accidentally pees, poops or throws up in the house you can clean it up right away before it starts to smell.
- Don't have to talk about someone behind anyone's back because they are not there.
- My bathroom is only 7 feet away. Don't have to share with coworkers.
- Can sit at your desk and dance and sing when your favorite song comes on.
- Can write a couple of personal e-mails during lunch break.
- If you pee or poop your pants, no one will know, just get a change of clothes.
- Can look up a phone or address on computer.
- Learn about new drug names on television or Internet.
- Can lie down for a migraine or eye strain.
- Boss is thousands of miles away. Can only contact you by e-mail or phone.
- Can laugh out loud and no one there to hear.
- Can pop a gross zit and no one will care.
- Can put a quick load of laundry in the washer or run and empty the dishwasher.
- Can burp and fart and you don't have to say excuse me.
- Can look on your phone view finder and see who is calling and ignore it.
- Can see who is on The Talk.
- Don't have to wear makeup if you don't want to or shampoo your hair.
- Can sing your favorite song out loud and out of key and no one laughs, not even your pets.

- Can get up and dance and no one will think you are acting strange.
- Can bitch about someone out loud and they won't get angry with you.
- Can play with the dog or cat a couple of minutes.
- Can stick fingers in your ears. There's a little ear wax in there.

CONS:

THERE ARE NONE!!! Only kidding.

- You sneeze and no one blesses you.
- Have to let the dog out to pee and poop and play.
- TV, refrigerator and bed are close by. You need to discipline yourself.
- Ringing in the ears constantly from having the headphones in. Mine sounds like water running through pipes. A ssss sound. I have to have a fan on when I go to bed so it drowns out the ringing.
- Have a bigger water, electric, healing and cooling bill because someone is home all day.
- You can't call off at your job and say my car broke down or say you will be late because the bus didn't show up.
- Hearing loss.
- If you start choking, you either have to do the Heimlich maneuver on yourself or run to the neighbor for help. You can't call 911.

Chapter 10

2-LINE RHYMES – Part 2

I went to the doctor for an anxiety attack,
He said just go home, you're a hypochondriac.

I don't feel any better because the doctor lowered my medication,
I better go back for another examination.

My gynecologist has me on hormone replacement therapy,
He said the next step will be psychotherapy.

I want to retire as a respected transcriptionist,
Because all while transcribing, I was a great perfectionist.

I've transcribed them often as a diagnosis,
But what exactly is sclerosis and stenosis.

I'm a transcriptionist, not a typist, I do so much more,
Call me a typist one more time and you're out the front door.

In college, I had to learn abbreviations, acronyms, and medical symbols,
I'm sorry, I thought they were talking about the musical cymbals.

I wrote a rhyme on what I thought was a long sheet of paper,
It turned out I was really using toilet paper.

I tried to spell a word on my cell but as it stands,
I can't enter otorhinolaryngologist with my man hands.

I'm writing these rhymes night and day with no break or hesitation,
I need to have the doctor check the dose on my medication.

Lori M. Radosny

My doctor told me to never cross my legs for a serious diagnosis,
He said it is possible to get deep venous thrombosis.

Brachial, cephalic, basilic, don't be alarmed,
They are just the names of veins in your arm.

Their credentials are impressive, MD, RN, CRNP, PA, MA and PhD,
They worked very hard to earn their degree.

I have aches in my wrist, what could it be from,
I scream with fear, is it carpal tunnel syndrome?

I got into the health care field because of a hot doctor on TV I'll never forget,
He taught me the word angiogram, his name was Chad Everett.

My great friend Jessie is a wise man that taught me to in order to survive,
To remember to live the dream every day and always, always keep hope alive.

Let us not forget the female rads for they are terrific,
But after looking at my reports, one of them said they are horrific.

It's 12:30 a.m., my work day is done, I have no strife,
They say if you love your job, you won't work a day in your life. (True)

I was born in 1961, it's really the year I'm telling thee,
I'm so old heck I remember watching Lawrence Welk on TV.

I still have some forgetfulness from my fall I say to you,
I missed my neurologist appointment today at a quarter to 2.

My job has an advantage that when I must pee,
I don't have to share the bathroom except for Dave and me.

I started these rhymes at age 53, Lori out loud cries,
I hope I can keep rhyming until the time of my demise.

Sir, I'm on Pittsburgh Today Live for being a rhyming inventor,
Please help me find KDKA, I think it's in Gateway Center.

I noticed a mole just above my left calf,
I'll call my dermatologist after I get my coffee and half and half.

I can't type numbers on the keyboard without taking a peek,
we must have learned them one day in school when I was "seek."

To all the outstanding dictators, let me declare, you voice is heaven sent,
I'm going to send an appreciation letter to the hospital president.

My teacher asked in college what are two fleshy folds which surround the mouth,
I took a guess and said lips so my scholarship wouldn't go south.

If I asked my gynecologist has he ever seen one too big or too small,
He might say to me, Lori, when you've seen one you've seen them all.

Sometimes I cry, want to give up, I compose myself and say what the ****,
Get your mind out of the gutter, I was going to say fire truck.

Transcriptionists like to go shopping, I'm showing respect,
One MT told me we need to get checked.

My job is stressful and can be jeopardizing,
Better take my blood pressure pill, mercury number is rising.

The attending physician makes his/her daily rounds,
To do this he must stay on the hospital grounds.

I went to the urologist because my urine was orange,

Uh-Oh, there's no rhyming word for the word orange!

It's not in my spell check, I can't find it anywhere,
Maybe they made that term up, it's more than I can bear.

To all health care professionals, your dedication is so appreciated,
We are all grateful for your skills are so sophisticated.

TIA, MVA, DJD, EKG, ACL, HTN, listen I said,
It's hard keeping all these abbreviations straight in my head.

I'm sitting at my desk here, thinkin' and thinkin',
Was that last patient's name really Abraham Lincoln?

Bronchoscopy, arthroscopy, even proctoscopy,
Anything is better than a colonoscopy.

I ordered a word book, I'm getting excited,
I'm in a hurry, I asked them to expedite it.

A machinist, a chemist, or exhibitionist,
No, I knew in high school, to be a transcriptionist.

Now I think I may have a UTI,
I have to pee I say with a sigh.

I transcribe and pay close attention but I am fearing,
after 33 years of transcribing I am getting hard of hearing.

Someone will say to me are you a typist, I yell from my windpipe,
I am a transcriptionist and I do not just type.

Chapter 11

RISKS OF BEING A MEDICAL TRANSCRIPTIONIST:

- I cannot hear in the presence of background noise. For example if I am watching something on TV and a big loud truck or motorcycle goes by I can't hear the TV until they have passed. I did some transcribing for an ear, nose and throat doctor. He taught me that.
- Eye strain.
- Neck strain.
- Carpal tunnel syndrome.
- Butt numbness and tingling.
- Arthritis in the hands.
- Shoulder tightness.
- Cramp in foot from using foot pedal.
- Back pain.

Chapter 12

THE DREADED "ARTHUR" AND OTHER PROBLEMS

There are three things that transcriptionists dread:

* Arthritis in the hands.

* Carpal Tunnel Syndrome.

* Any abnormality dealing with your transcribing foot (used on the foot pedal).

I have had degenerative joint disease in my knees for about the last 3-4 years. I need to have surgery but I am trying to put it off for the time being. I'm exercising by dancing and using weights. I have trouble getting up and down steps. Other than that I can walk pretty well.

I stopped taking my ibuprofen for my knees for a little while because some of my labs were abnormal. I noticed that since being off of it, my joints in my hands are now hurting. I'm back on the medicine and hope that it will take care of the pain.

Another thing that concerns a medical transcriptionist is carpal tunnel syndrome. This can happen at any time and is extremely painful. I haven't had symptoms of that so far...thank goodness!

The other thing that a medical transcriptionist is anything dealing with your transcribing foot, i.e. cramping, drop foot, numbness, bunion, etc.

Chapter 13

RITUALS:

Transcriptionists are a lot like baseball players and radiologists. We have our rituals we do as we go through our work day.

For example, when the baseball player comes up to bat:

- Digs his foot a little in the dirt in the batter's box.
- Some players cross themselves. I think this is beautiful.
- Looks to 3rd base coach for the sign.
- Takes a practice swing.
- Adjusts helmet.
- Spits.
- Tightens his batting gloves, adjusting the Velcro.
- Are there 1 or 2 outs and who is on base.
- Makes a quick check of the jock, making sure everything is in place down there. Makes adjustments as necessary.
- Finally gets in hitting stance.
- Wait, calls time.
- Steps out of batter's box.
- Takes a quick peek at the blond in the third row.
- Then he starts the ritual all over again.
- That's only one batter. No wonder baseball takes so long.

When a transcriptionist comes into work:

- Puts beverage on desk in a spot so it won't spill.
- Takes any medication as needed. Especially the high blood pressure and anxiety pills.

- Sits in chair and makes sure the height is good. Adjusts as necessary. Is my butt located in the center? Ahh, that feels good right there.
- Adjusts keyboard position. It has to be located just in the middle of your body or it doesn't feel right and it is uncomfortable to type with a crooked keyboard.
- Takes out a mirror to see what hair looks like, and see if there is anything in your teeth.
- Move hair away from your face.
- Adjusts the monitor to make sure it is the right height, front and center.
- Takes out earphones out of drawer, put them in your ears.
- Take off right shoe, get a better feel for the pedal especially if you wear high heels. The only problem is your right sock wears out faster than your left because of pressing the pedal so many times in one shift. Check watch, break is in two hours. Lunch in four hours. I'll have the fish. Put on some hand lotion. Maybe some lip gloss. Want to look nice. Talk to the transcriptionist next to you to see what he/she did last evening.
- Start typing.

The radiologists do this as their ritual:

I love radiologists because as their ritual they develop sort of a checklist they probably learned when they were learning Radiology in school. And after a while, the Rad (Radiologist for short) develops his/her way of dictating. They usually go in a certain order for each type of study they dictate.

Chapter 14

2-LINE RHYMES – Part 3

Oh no, my computer crashed, I see the dreaded blue screen,
but not to worry, I calmly count to seventeen.

While transcribing, there's always surprises.
Don't forget to do your hand and finger exercises.

Treat your hands with tenderness and care,
for they are our moneymakers, that's why we have a pair.

The dictator dictates about poop, thanks a bunch!
Because I just got back from taking my lunch.

I am grateful I'm a radiology transcriptionist because in this regard,
I tried acute care transcription and it is really hard!

Sometimes while transcribing I have to scratch my head and sigh,
but when a doctor says something funny I have to stop and slap my
thigh.

I'm glad I work at home, no traffic, no good clothes to wear,
I can wear my slippers. Oh goodness did I put on underwear?

I didn't make my line count today I say with sorrow,
but don't worry I'll do better tomorrow.

The transcriptionist bond is strong and secure,
we help each other, depend on one another, we have no fear.
I try to type everything to the letter,
as a transcriptionist I can only get learn and get better and better.

Lori M. Radosny

After I typed my first Rad report I did truly sing
"Love Is A Many Splendored Thing."

I missed my calling because I didn't know it,
I should have become a literary poet.

I start this poem by saying it is not in jest,
but there are some things I need to get off my chest.

I am getting a little messy on the keyboard, I need to trim my nails,
but first I must get out those important e-mails.

I still can't understand how to do a macro,
Beverly F. tried to teach me but I said holy mackerel.

Some Rads say something is nonspecific, that I have seen,
But what exactly does nonspecific really mean.

For the fast talkers my earphones I must put down,
They talk as though they are hurrying to catch the last bus out of town.

For the less than best dictators I want to swear
but I simply smile and wait for retirement and Medicare.

I never know how to spell cysticercosis,
instead couldn't they just use tuberculosis?

On no, I put in an extra comma. Really? Pl-ease.
Please don't report me to the transcription police!

To the doctors who say thank you at the end of a dictation.
I know they appreciate our hard work and dedication.

Oh my heavens, for goodness sakes,
why don't some Rads give the study dates.

What is the difference between a lesion and a mass,
I should have paid attention in anatomy class.

Do you really know when to use flair and flare?
These words come up often so learn which to put where.

I just typed on a report that the bladder is full and don't you know,
to the bathroom I trot, I hope it's a steady flow.

My letters on my keyboard are mostly rubbed off,
I try to find the letter M but can only scoff.

As I pick up my cell phone and give it a tap,
I see with great joy it had a rhyming app,

People have told me I am in an important profession,
I smile back at them with a thankful expression.

At times I get words that I get that are a real zingers,
So I raise my right hand and salute with one of my fingers.

The first computer was a UNIVA1 and sold to US Census Bureau on 3/31/1951.
Heck, I was at a great advantage, they perfected it by the time I was born in 1961.

Am I talented or maybe brilliant,
you can tell me I'm pretty resilient.

If you understand what I'm explaining,
Please chime in, I promise not to be a pain.

To concentrate better, I cut out the bourbon,
I should have listened to my dad and remained a virgin.

I take a break to clear my head, rest my fingers,

But the pain and ache in them still lingers.

All this rhyme writing has me in a tizzy,
I should see a neurologist because now I am totally dizzy.

Telephone rings, I recognize who is calling, HR, my employment status is changed.
Maybe I'll move to New York and get a job on the floor of the stock exchange.

Chapter 15

SOME TRANSCRIPTION STORIES:

There is a doctor I transcribe. He has a very strong and stern-sounding voice. If he says the lungs are clear, THE DAMN LUNGS ARE CLEAR!!!!! Only kidding.

Some Rads are very helpful. They will spell words while doing their dictations and we MT's (Medical Transcriptionists) are very appreciative for that.

At a doctor's office was the nicest urologist you would ever want to meet. He was always very kind to me and he is an excellent dictator. He called me Lori P. because at one point there were two of us named Lori in the office. I asked him in an e-mail how he liked my work and he said, "Lori you were and always will be a great transcriptionist." Thank you Dr. RJM. You were always my favorite dictator in the office.

The worst thing that can happen to a radiologist is ---→ laryngitis. I can tell right away if they have it or even if they aren't feeling well. You can pick this up just by their voice. But I give credit to them as they still come to work and always do a great job even when they don't feel well.

I like to try and guess if by the Rads voice if they are good looking. A game I like to play.

Chapter 16

A TRANSCRIPTIONIST'S PRAYER:

Dear Lord,

Please bless our radiologists today as they work very hard every day to give their findings and impressions so they can provide other physicians with diagnoses on how to treat conditions and cure patients of their ailments.

Please help me to realize that their work is very important and they should be very proud of the jobs they perform on a daily basis. It is an important task in the hospital setting and they do it so well. I know I poked some fun at them in this book so please forgive me. I really understand how important they are to us.

Amen.

The Personal Part:

Chapter 17

MY MOM AND DAD

First I think it is pretty cool. My mom and dad had the same birthday along with an uncle in the family, January 17th. My dad was 4 years older than my mom. They got married when my mom was 19 and my dad was 23.

I had really loving parents. My mom would do anything for her kids. She was a great knitter and whenever anyone had a baby she would knit them the cutest little baby afghans. She was the best cook. She made the best pierogies from scratch. She made the ones with sauerkraut and ricotta cheese. These were my favorite. One time my brother, Bob, ate 12 of them at one sitting.

We baby-sat for my cousin's son once in a while. He came over one time when we had pierogies and my mom gave him some. He's eating and my mom asked how are they, he said "delicious." He wasn't more than 3 at the time. My mom and I looked at each other saying how did he know that big word?

After dinner at home, my brothers or I would go into the kitchen and say to mom, Mom, I'm hungry. She would say – Kitchen's closed. Eat some cereal. And we did. She cracked her gum in high school. One teacher said – MARY, SPIT THAT GUM OUT! My mom loved Bobby Vinton the singer because he was Polish. Remember, Roses are red my love, violets are blue; sugar is sweet my love, but not as sweet as you. She also was so proud when Pope John Paul II became a Pope because he also was Polish.

Picture it. September 3, 1961. A future Transcriptionist Extraordinaire is born. My parents were going to name me Celeste which is a pretty cool name. The story goes that my mom was in the hospital after having me and she was watching TV. On some show's credits, the name Lori Maria was showing on the screen. She fell in love with the name and gave it to me. If you ask someone named Lori their birthday, most likely they were born in the 60's or 70's.

Her two sisters died. My mom died about 5 months after my Aunt Annie due to cancer. I think my mother saw that and gave up hope. My Aunt Lottie died young about 39 years old. Very sad. I really don't remember her but I saw pictures of her and she was very beautiful. She had 3 children who were very young. It was sad to see them go through that. Mom had cancer of the lung and I smoked. Everyone would tell me to quit smoking but I didn't listen. You have to be ready to quit or you'll go right back to it. I remember it was September 28th 5 years ago that I quit. I was ready. I started getting concerned because I smoked for 30 years, ages 18 to 48. I started thinking about mom and how she suffered. I said to myself that I didn't want to give Sweetie (our dog at the time) and Dave second hand smoke. I said I'll just try for a day and it went well. Really didn't have withdrawal symptoms. I tried the patch which didn't work for me. I used the gum and that did the trick. My mom was in the hospital a lot but it finally happened that they couldn't do anything further for her. My dad was planning to have hospice care and was making arrangements. She came home. She was in bed most of the time and my dad took loving care of her. My dad went to check on her and she had died. He came down and said your mother died. I panicked and said go check again (why I don't know). I swore I heard her call my name. He did and came down and said she died. My dad wasn't sure who to call so he called our local funeral home. They said to call the police and they would help him take care of it. She wasn't looking too well when she was sick, the cancer took its toll. The funeral home did a wonderful job. She looked beautiful and her hair looked perfect. The way I remembered her when she wasn't sick. The mom I always loved. We picked out a pretty dress for her to wear. When we said our final goodbyes, I wanted to put something in the casket that meant a lot to me the way she did. I finally decided on my high school class ring.

My mom could catch a fly with her hand. She would cup her hand and grab it. A couple times she missed but eventually caught it. She wouldn't kill the fly but let it free outside. Talk about not hurting a fly.

My mom had her sayings. She would say to Bobby, shake a leg, the bus is coming. She also said – If you don't know, you don't know, you know????

At Thanksgiving at our house, everyone would gather for dinner and my mom did all the cooking by herself. After she brought out the food, she would sit in the kitchen and eat by herself. My Aunt Annie would say Mame, c'mon in here and eat with us. She wouldn't do it.

When I was very little, one time my mom was making me a bottle to drink. I was on the couch waiting for it. All of a sudden I hear a crash. I went up to the kitchen and my mom was holding the broken bottle. That was how she got me to go off the bottle. I thought that it was the only one in the world so I didn't have a bottle after that.

My dad. What can I say. He was amazing too. He loved his kids and also would do anything for them. He many times rode me to work and picked me up when I was done so I wouldn't have to wait for a bus in the snow. He was in World War II and received 4 bronze medals. He was a good typist and the Army wanted him to be a typist here in the US. He said, no I want to go to the war. He was an interpreter in Germany because he could speak Polish fluently. He said one time there were about 100 men in his troop. Everyone got killed but him and another man. My dad said he could see his Guardian Angel on his shoulder protecting him. After he died I received a beautiful letter about dad being in the service and how he served his country from President Obama.

My dad got a job in the steel mill which he loved. He got laid off because the steel industry was doing terribly at the time. He took odd jobs to pay the bills and provide for his family. I am very proud of him for doing that. A very loving man. They say girls want to grow up and marry a man just like their dad. I was meant to meet because Dave is very much like my dad in my eyes, strong, loving, caring, and generous. My dad loved Dave very much. He said to Dave while in the nursing home do one thing for Lori, make her happy. Dave promised he would and has kept his promise for the last 25 years.

Before my dad died he always said he wanted to be cremated. He didn't want to be buried in the cold ground. After he died, my brother, Bob, wanted to bury him in a veteran's cemetery. I thought this was a terrific idea. My dad was proud of being in the Army. He told many war stories that we never tired of hearing. I think he's happy where is now laid to rest. Miss him dearly. Love you, Dad. Mom, too.

I love men that can dance well. I think I get that from my dad. My mother and my dad loved to dance to polkas. They would go to clubs and dance the night away. When I danced a polka with him, he would twirl me around, it was like heaven on earth. It was so much fun. I was his little girl then and I always will be. I could get a job where I watch people dance and I would be just as happy as a lark. I love TV shows where people dance. American Bandstand, Soul Train (yes I go back that far), and Dancing With The Stars.

One more story about my dad. I loved Jerry Lewis in his early movies with Dean Martin. My dad couldn't take him sometimes because Jerry was so silly. Jerry was the only one that could make me laugh. I would be watching a movie and my mom said that it's time to go to bed. I said, Mum, can't I watch a little more of Jerry Lewis? She said Jerry Lewis doesn't have to get up for school tomorrow, you do! She had a point that I couldn't argue with so I went to bed. I saw Jerry Lewis recently on The Talk. He is still funny and still making me laugh. He looks terrific. I would always watch him every year on the Labor Day Telethons he did. I stayed up as late as I could keep my eyes open and go to bed, and then watch it some more the next day. I love him dearly for bringing laughter into my life and for giving me a sense of humor. I think that's why I am such a character today, I take after Jerry.

After my mom died and dad was alone in the house I would check on him. I went in the house, went into the living room and he was sleeping on the couch and had a paper towel over his eyes. I said hi dad, he didn't answer. I yelled a little louder, still no response. Finally I yelled DAD. He jumped and said What? I thought the worst happened.

Dad always wanted a pickup truck. After mom died, he finally got his wish. He bought a light blue pickup truck. That was his baby. I would say I'll drive us somewhere, he said – We'll take my pickup.

I called my dad to ask him what his social security number was for some papers I had to fill out. He was in the nursing home. He rattled off some numbers and I said that's only seven numbers. He was telling me his military ID number. It was amazing that he could remember that still after 66 years.

My father, Walter Radosny, Sr., will be honored in his hometown as a war hero. A banner will be lifted with his Army picture. He will be honored for his service in the Army and the things that he endured while there. Again, a World War II hero that is worthy of such praise as are all veterans of all of the wars who served their country for us to be safe now as well as in the past.

I would like to thank my Uncle Yosty and Aunt Jeanne for all they did while my dad was in the nursing home. I will be forever grateful for what you did for him. Thank you for taking him to doctor's appointments and all the visiting you did with him. Anytime I asked if you could do something for him you would do it. I am glad that you were with my dad when he died. I am glad he had family there while Bob and I left the nursing home and then returned to find he had died. Thank you always.

Chapter 18

MY BIG BROTHER BOB

My brother Bob is really cool. He went to college at the University of Pittsburgh for Journalism. He worked in various newspapers when he finished school. He eventually got a job in our local liquor store. He was there about 30 years and retired a year or two ago. He writes articles for a major newspaper in Pittsburgh. Excellent journalist. He believes in saving the environment. We save newspapers for him and every week he picks them up to be recycled. He says thanks to us for saving a tree. He tells us ways to save energy and save the planet. He was kind enough to lend us money to buy a dryer when it broke and a new computer when ours crashed and wasn't able to be fixed. When I talk to him on the phone about a problem I have, he always gives good advice. He kindly emptied out Walt's apartment after Walt died and that was a big chore. Virgos like to shop. Bob used to write my English papers. He was a writer. I said don't make it sound too great. Make it sound like a 10th grader wrote it. He loves writing. This has been his passion and it shows when he writes a newspaper article. He lives in a town near me and is helping to build up the town. He is even writing plays. He is a very talented man.

I was very thankful that Bob was with me when my dad died. I don't think I could have gone through that alone. I love you, Bob.

When Bob was about a year old he won a cute baby contest in our local paper at the time. He was really cute. But he's not cute anymore. Now he's handsome!

Dave had the flu really severe and he went to the hospital by ambulance because I was working. I called Bob and asked if he would pick up Dave when he was done in the ER. Dave wasn't done until midnight and Bob went to the hospital to pick Dave up. I will be forever grateful to Bob for this. I won't forget what you do for us.

He has two wonderful sons named Erick and Kevin. I never really got to see them much when they were young but I saw them when they came to my dad's funeral that they turned out to be fine young men.

Bob has a beautiful granddaughter named Madison. She is a very pretty little girl and is very considerate of others. A classmate in school can't go out for recess due to a chronic health condition so Madison will sit with him in school and play board games. She is also very bright and likes to read books. Bob sends her books to read every so often. She calls it the Father Bob Book Club.

Below is an e-mail I received from Bob when I asked him what battles our dad fought in during the war. Also he talks about his granddaughter, Madison.

They never told you where you were. You just fought. As per his medals, he fought in Normandy after the D-Day invasion, in the Battle of the Bulge, the Rhineland, the battle of Achen, a German city, and part of the battle for the Hurtgen Forest. He really shouldn't have volunteered to go into combat. His typing skills would have kept him out, but he wanted to go "where the action was." He saw plenty of that. After his first day, he said, maybe "I should have thought about this a little more." German cannons, the 88's, will do that.

Madison called it the Father Bob Book Club. Erick is ok with that, who is, of course, her real father. It's a name she just came up with, and I like it. I love that little girl. I'll do anything for her.

Chapter 19

MY MAIN MAN, DAVE

I decided on joining a bowling league on Friday nights. There I met Dave. I thought he was really super cute and funny. Dave is my rock. I was always worried at my one job that I would get fired. Every day I talked to Dave and said that doctor is going to fire me. He said, the doctor isn't going to fire you. The doctor never did. Dave always knows how to calm me down when I'm upset about something.

The bowling league I joined was so much fun. We had a good group. Always had a really fun time every week. I was laughing more than I was bowling and really enjoying myself.

Dave wanted to ask me out but he was afraid, why I don't know. I think he was afraid of me rejecting him. He finally did and we went out to dinner. It just happened to be my birthday. When I dropped him off at home he said "Happy Birthday Lori," and patted my shoulder a couple of times. He wasn't sure if he should kiss me or not.

We talked for hours on the phone all the time. He said he liked hearing my sexy telephone voice. He has one too. I asked him to go with me to my high school 10 year reunion in 1989. He went and we are still together 25 years later. We are very happy together. He makes me laugh all the time. He likes to quote lines from old TV shows. He's a very smart man. He's a very bright man.

We aren't married. We talked about it maybe only once or twice in the 25 years together. I didn't mind. I have my Boo. I think he was scared that I would do something. His dad died after a bout with esophageal cancer. Ten months later Dave came home to find his mother had died of a heart attack in the family room. He said he felt a shiver go down his spine earlier that day and knew something was wrong. Dave proved to me after that he was a strong man. He had to take care of all the things regarding the house, her will, taking care of arrangements, and many other things. He was an only child and I hope I helped him through his loss. After his mother died, I think he was lonely and missed his mom and dad very much. He asked me to move in with him. He handed me a list that he would do my laundry, cook for me and some other cute things. I said I would. That was about 10 years ago. I have been happy for the total 25 years and especially the last 10. I love being with him every day. He is my first love and will be my only love. I can't wait until he comes from work every day. He calls me from work every day at 10 am, 12 noon and 2 pm to see how Sullivan and I are doing. I think he's always afraid that I will leave him for someone else. I always tell him I'm not leaving you for anybody but I think he still worries a little. When we first met he went through a terrible breakup. We understand each other, know when the other is upset about something. We always cheer each other up when we are sad. We have had little tiffs but we always make up 10 minutes later. We can't be mad at each other for very long.

We don't make a lot of money but we are still very happy together. We do what we can to make ends meet, paying the bills, etc. We share a checking account and at one point our balance was $1.56. Dave worries about money, taking care of the house, making me happy (which I always am), keeping everything together. He does a great job.

I remember when we had our first "romantic session." We went out for our first Valentine's Day. I made him wait 5 months for the special event. Let's just say I never had a romantic session before because he was my first boyfriend. I was 28. Then on February 17th, it happened. Happy ever since. Every February 17th is a very special anniversary for us both. I'll never forget that day ever. It was funny because at the hospital where I worked at the time, there was a girl who asked me did you do it yet? I said no. She said do like Nike says, "just do it!" I went in one day and left her a note on her desk. It read "Just like Nike, I did it!"

Dave is my electronic repair man. I am electronic device illiterate. I can barely dial a phone number to make a telephone call. I hate when things don't work as they are intended to work. When there's something wrong with the computer I yell hysterically DAVE COME HERE, THIS COMPUTER IS ****** UP AGAIN. And he always fixes it. Computer, fax machine, cell phone, E-reader device, he can fix them all.

Dave calls me Literal Lori. One day I was down in the basement and he asked me to bring up a towel. It's in the laundry basket he said. I said okay. I brought up the towel. He asked why didn't you bring up the laundry basket. I said you only asked for the towel.

We talk about everything and anything no matter how simple or silly. He's a great conversationalist. He loves saying quotes from All In The Family. Dave puts ketchup on everything. He said Archie once said after Gloria asked him why he was putting ketchup on something odd. Archie said I'd put ketchup on a donut if it needed it, little goil. He also watches The Three Stooges and can recite lines before Curly, Larry and Moe say them, he's seen them so many times. He can also recite lines from the movies Night Shift and The Godfather. We love watching Night Shift because Michael Keaton is in it and he is from Pittsburgh (Yayyy).

I always asked God to send me a man that makes me laugh and happy. It took 28 years but God came through and gave me Dave. I think I was meant to join that bowling league. God smiled upon me that day in 1989. I really feel he had a plan for me. I am thankful every day that Dave is in my life. I call him my Boo-Boo. He is my Boo-Boo forever. I love you baby!

Dave will say words like flatulence, renal failure and subchondral hematoma. I said where did you learn those words? He said, M*A*S*H*.

Dave puts things he gets in the mail in great big cardboard boxes. When he is looking for something it might take him 4 hours but he will keep looking until he finds it. And he does find it. That's the amazing part!

Chapter 20

A TRIBUTE TO MY BROTHER WALT:

I always said that my brother, Walt, and I were like twins born 13 years apart. He was born September 12, 1948 and I was born September 3, 1961. We looked exactly alike. We were both Virgos, perfectionists and listened to people talk for a living. He was a court reporter. We loved to go shopping, smoked like crazy and had many other things in common. When we went shopping, he would wait patiently while I looked at the purses and jewelry I didn't need. When we came home from shopping, we would tell each other about our purchases. I found a tie to match those blue pants on the sale rack. Yeah, I said, I found the perfect purse. Like the 60 previous purses I had were no longer perfect.

Walt was my Santa Claus. He made the holiday extra special. He always got so excited about Christmas. Every year he would buy me the most beautiful gifts. I couldn't wait until he came home for the holiday and see all the wrapped packages he bought me, anxiously waiting until I could open them. After we opened our presents, we would sit and talk about how we found this or that present for each other.

I would call him often. He lived in Meadville, PA. I would ask his advice about things and just talk about anything.

Walt adored Barbra Streisand, loved her voice and songs that she sang. He would go home after a stressful day at work and listen to her sing. He had every album she ever made. I brought them home with me after he died. He went to Las Vegas to see her in concert. I only wish that he was able to meet her in person.

Walt died March 4, 2006 after having a hip replacement. He was in the hospital and wanted to go home. He developed a serious infection in the hospital and the doctor told him many times to stay in the hospital so the infection could be treated. He wanted to go home anyway. I know my brother, he wanted to go home so he could smoke. He couldn't smoke while in the hospital. They discharged him against medical advice. I called him about 5-6 times that day at his apartment with no answer. I thought well he's probably hobbling around and can't get to the phone. Finally I was worried and called his best friend, Elsie, and asked her to go check on him. She lived a distance from Walt and asked his landlord to go and check on him. Walt had died. Elsie called and gave me the bad news. We were in total shock, as would be expected. We had to go to Meadville and make arrangements and say goodbye.

Walt was my best friend next to Dave. I was just sorry I wasn't with him when he died. I wished I could have been there with him. I miss him still to this day. Dave and I talk of Walt about all the funny things he said and did. I had to go to work on one of his visits. I came home. He said, so how was your day? I said it was good. Three seconds later he said again, so how was your day? Too funny.

Walt was the early bird and I liked to sleep until noon. I think this was the only thing different about us. I always slept on the couch when he visited me and he slept in my bed. He would wake me up and say, Wake up Lori, time to greet the brand new day!

Walt was in his 50s when he had to learn a new computer system at work. He was born in 1948 and wasn't quite interested in learning the system. He would call me totally aggravated and said that computer system was dumb. I told him to hang in there, it would get better and it did. He finally caught on. I am the same way. It was hard for me to learn the new electronic health record system at the doctor's office where I worked.

He was a court reporter. He had a transcript he wanted me to look at because it was a medical case. As I read, it said that the patient had a staff infection. I told Walt it should be spelled Staph infection. He was so upset that he had made an error on the transcript. That was because he was a perfectionist, like me (see the twins thing?)

Walt did very considerate things for people. If you called him and told him something that made you sad, he would send you a cheer-up card. He went to the bank one time and the woman who worked there helped him with his banking. He went back about 20 minutes later with a little plant thanking her for her help. We were in a card store one time and he struck up a conversion with the person in line behind us. When we left the store he said, "I made a new friend today."

Walt had some problems. He developed psoriasis and got it all over his body. He was worried that he would get it on his face but it didn't. He tried some therapies for it but gave up. I think with some forms of psoriasis your immune system gets compromised. Maybe that's why he developed the infection while in the hospital. He had testicular cancer twice and had to take radiation therapy. He was treated for alcoholism. He went to rehab once in this far-away place. My dad and I went to see him. I don't know how we found it. Walt said he would come home from work about 6 pm and drink 12 beers before he went to bed. He thought this was normal. He went through all of these things and still had a happy attitude and was always smiling.

One Thanksgiving we had it at my apartment and Walt came home. He came in the door and I said, "Where's the turkey?" He said that I thought you were getting it. So instead of turkey we all had spaghetti.

Walt always joked that he had OCD. He would wash his hands 10-12 times a day. He would only dry his face with a while towel.

Everyone at work called him Mr. GQ. He always dressed well with a new suit, new tie and everything was coordinated.

Walt always said he wanted to write a book about his experiences in court. But he never got to do that. I think he is the reason I am writing this book. He is talking to me from heaven.

Walt took me to see the plays Cats and Phantom of the Opera. I'll never forget that.

We were at the funeral home for Walt and someone who looked like he might be a homeless man came to see Walt. No doubt, Walt must have done something for him or helped him out in some way.

Walt could memorize a lot of phone numbers in his head. Someone at work would say – What is that attorney's phone number? I guess he was their telephone directory.

After he died I went to Meadville and drove his car to Pittsburgh. It got repossessed because I didn't make any further payments. His license plate said "HEUTHR" which in court reporting means "hi there." The man who took the car called me to make the arrangements. I asked him to save me the license plate and put it in our mailbox. He said he would but he never did. I was so sad about that.

Walt spoke Polish well. He was around my mom, dad, aunts, uncles, grandmothers and grandfathers who were here and some of them could only speak Polish. Walt was proud to be Polish.

The boy could eat and he was never really heavy but only a little. One time he came to visit. For breakfast he had 6 pancakes, 10 strips of bacon, hash browns and 5 cups of coffee. He loved buffets and salad bars. Heck, you can take as much as you want.

Walt and I loved the TV show, The Nanny. It is in reruns now on TV. I watch it and laugh and think about Walt. I think Walt like Fran because she admired Barbra Streisand so much.

If Walt or my Aunt Annie saw a crooked picture on the wall, they had to fix it. If you had a little dandruff on your shoulders, they would have to brush it off. Walt hung out a lot with my Aunt Annie and Uncle Buck. They would drive up to Meadville for visits when Walt was young. That's when Walt fell in love with the town. He was offered a court reporting job in Pittsburgh that paid $60,000 a year. That was a lot of money in the 60s. He took a lower paying position because he wanted to live in Meadville.

Every Memorial Day and Veteran's Day, when they play the Star Spangled Banner or Taps on a TV show marking the occasion, he would start crying. I'm the same way. I think we both realized what my dad went through in World War II.

If Walt left the kitchen to go the family room and forgot his cigarettes in the kitchen he would say – If I used my head I wouldn't have to use my feet so much. Think about it.

He could never pronounce the word cinnamon. It always came out as cinnamon-namon-namon. Too funny.

He would always compliment people whether it be what you were wearing, a new haircut or if you got a new pair of glasses.

I wrote a lot about Walt in this book. I wanted to tell everyone to tell everybody that you love them whenever you see them or talk to them on the phone. You never know when that person will be taken from you in an instant. I gave Walt a hard time sometimes. I think we were so much alike that I saw me in him. I feel that God punished me for being mean. And now I am paying the price because Walt was taken from me when he was only 57. I have always said that God punishes people for the bad things they do to other people.

Chapter 21

DAVE'S MOM AND DAD:

I was picking up Dave and we were going to the movies. I parked in front of the house and he waved me to come in. Uh-oh I had never met his parents before that time. So I go in, sit down and his mother is at the kitchen table and she says hi and I say hi. I'm thinking what can I say? Dave told me one time she was a good bowler. So I said, Dave says you are a good bowler. She smiled and said something like I try my best. Her highest bowling series was 600, her highest single game was 237. Pretty impressive!

His dad was a salesman for a cruise ship company. Dave says he was a master salesman. He was away on business a lot and it would only be Dave and his mom. We had fun times. His mother also had a great sense of humor. Dave always tells me stories about his mom and dad and I never get tired of hearing them.

Dave's mom was an avid reader. She could read three novels at one time and keep all the story lines straight in her head. She could also do the New York Times puzzle in pen. That's also pretty impressive, don't you think?

Later I asked Dave if his parents liked me. They said – You got a keeper.

Dave's mom was orphaned when she was about 9 years old. Her mother and father both died of pneumonia. She was raised by her Aunt Margaretta (Marshy). We have pictures of both his mother and her brother when they were young. We also have a picture of his mom when she graduated high school. She was a very stunning woman. Even when she was in her older years, she didn't have a wrinkle on her face. Still beautiful.

Chapter 22

MY GRANDMOTHER ON MY FATHER'S SIDE:

Below is an excerpt from my Uncle Sam's (my dad's brother) book regarding the Radosny Family History. It is about my grandmother, who we called Busha, and what she would cook for the family.

There were other Polish dishes which Mother made on occasion which I remember to this day. "Czarnina" was duck's blood soup, made, as the name implies, with the blood of a freshly killed duck. Mother would slit the duck's throat and catch the blood in a basin. This she would cook with prunes, celery, onions and vinegar and would serve this black soup with boiled whole potatoes. I think only she and Pap (my grandfather) ate this soup.

Below is an excerpt from the same book above regarding the time my father had pneumonia when he was young and how they treated him at home.

When the doctors said that Walter (my dad), suffering from double pneumonia, was not likely to survive the illness, Mother mustered the family to gather and heat building bricks in the oven and deliver them to her. She wrapped the heated bricks in blankets and rags and packed them around Walter as he lay in bed. She also prepared a mustard plaster which she placed on his chest and back, and by morning, the fever had broken. Walter still bears the burn marks from the mustard plasters, but he survived the ordeal and grew strong and well enough to serve in the Infantry in World War II.

Thank you for the information, Uncle Sam.

Chapter 23

SWEETIE AND SULLIVAN, OUR PET STORIES:

We had a beagle mix named Sweetie who was abused by her previous owner. We got her at the Humane Society about 11 years ago. When we saw her there, she was barking so loud and furious as if to say PICK ME, PICK ME, PICK ME. Well didn't we fall in love with her right there and then. She died on July 12th of last year of congestive heart failure.

I talked to Sweetie like she was a person. I went to Sweetie to tell her I had a doctor's appointment and was getting ready. She sat up and smiled at me. I went to tell her I was leaving for the doctor's appointment and will see her in a little bit. She didn't move. I touched her a little to wake her up thinking she was sleeping. When I saw her tongue I new something was wrong. I called Dave screaming SWEETIE DIED. SHE'S NOT RESPONDING. SHE'S NOT RESPONDING TO ME. I asked him to come home right now. He called a few minutes later and said he was on his way. We both cried at the front door. We finally went into our office where she always slept. Dave covered her with an old sheet and carried her to the car and we took her to be cremated. The Vet made an impression on some sort of clay of her paw. I thought that was so thoughtful for the Vet to do. Also he sent us the most beautiful sympathy card signed by everyone in the office. That card was very special to us.

Dave and I cried for three days because she really was a sweetie. I hope we provided her with a happy home and I think we did that. I was sad that she died alone. We have many happy and funny memories of her. Dave and I always tell Sweetie stories. And when we are sad and crying about her we say we just had a "Sweetie moment."

She had a doggie door on the garage door and she went out whenever she wanted. She was very territorial. One day she came up the steps. I looked over and she killed a possum. That possum was heavy. At least 15 pounds. I don't know how she got that possum through her doggie door, carried it up 12

steps to show it to me. She was very proud. The poor possum had his eyes closed and had his mouth open a little. He must have just been to the dentist because he had the whitest teeth I ever saw on an animal. I called Dave frantically at work. What should I do? He said put it in a garbage bag and put it outside so it doesn't smell. I said okay. I got a large garbage bag and broom and tried to roll the possum into the bag. Finally after several tries. Success. I put it out on the front porch till Dave came home.

Well along comes Sullivan. We went to the Humane Society and didn't see any dogs we liked or the ones we did like were unavailable. Dave and I went home disappointed. Online we checked out this dog named Sullivan. His family left him alone in the house and never came back. The neighbors heard him barking and thankfully called the Humane Society to rescue him. We both said at the same time on the phone, did you see that dog named Sullivan? Dave went to the shelter to see about him but he was already adopted by someone else. We again were disappointed. By chance, Dave called the shelter again the next day and they said that Sullivan was available again. The family who adopted him brought him back. Dave called and told me that. I said I have to get there fast before someone else adopts him. I called my friend, Jessie, to take me to the Humane Society because I don't like driving in Pittsburgh. When I got to the shelter I timidly said that I'm here to see Sullivan, hoping he wasn't already adopted as it is on a first come, first serve basis. I went to a little porch so I could meet him. He was so energetic and playful. I said I'm in love, I'll take him. We adopted him! The girl said he had kennel cough and bronchitis and was recently neutered. They said to give him antibiotics for the bronchitis. He brought up a lot of phlegm on the rug but we didn't mind, he was sick and we just cleaned it up. I think that is why the people before us brought him back, he was making a mess. He got all better.

He is the sweetest pooch next to Sweetie anyone can have. He likes to meet new people and is very friendly. If I am upset and crying about something sad, he comes to me and gives me kisses. If I make a loud noise somewhere in the house, he comes to check on me to make sure I'm okay. He wakes Dave up every morning at 4:30 on the dot. Sullivan and Dave like to play ball. Sullivan tears up socks, bras, underwear and blankets. We don't mind. We will give him a good home like we did Sweetie. We hope he is happy to be with us and I truly think he is. We can see it in his cute little thankful face.

Whenever I take a nap during the day, Sullivan will come on the bed and nap with me. I tell Sullivan I'm going to take a nap. He immediately follows me into the bedroom. He is protecting me.

Names I call Sullivan: Sweetheart, honey, baby doll, cute poochie, Sully, Bubba, little Boo-Boo, pup, little munchkin, punkin or Su-Su. He answers to them all.

If you leave the bathroom door open a little and are peeing, Sullivan will come in and watch you. A couple of times I said I have to poop and I don't think you want to be in here for this. He then walks away. Smart pooch.

When Dave scolds Sullivan for something, Sullivan will turn his back to Dave. He does it all the time. It is too cute. He doesn't do it to me.

Around his eyes, there are dark lines all around them. It looks like he is wearing eyeliner. He is such a sweet pooch.

I will ask Sullivan if he wants a treat. He will bark and I give him one. I ask him, do you want a knuckle sandwich? I would never hit him. I don't believe in hitting animals, but it's just cute the way he looks at me.

I was talking to Dave on the phone recently. I put him on speaker and he said hello to Sullivan. Sullivan is looking at the phone, then all over the room and then he ran to the front door to see if Dave was there. I said I would never do that to him again. Poor pooch.

Chapter 24

MY COUSIN, JOHNNY

Johnny is an amazing man. He married his wife Bonnie and they have four beautiful children. He can put together anything for you. He built my desk I am using right now. He put together my elliptical machine with no sweat. He also put our lawn mower together. I think I mentioned in another part of my book that they had their first daughter, Valeri, on Valentine's Day. That's why they named her Valeri. I think that is so sweet!

One time when we were young teenagers and we were at my old house talking in the driveway. Practically every car that went by honked and they waved to Johnny. It was so funny. He knows everybody. You can never have enough friends.

He calls me "cuz" and I call him "Jasiu" pronounced Yushu, which is Polish for John. He went to an elderly Polish woman's house to do some work at her house during his job one day. He said she seemed very sad and was eating a piece of toast. She asked Johnny his name and he said "Jasiu." He said she smiled from ear to ear. I told Johnny that you made her day. He's very considerate that way.

When Walt died, Johnny, his wife, Bonnie, and my Uncle Buck came all the way up to Meadville for the funeral. They didn't have to do that but Johnny said that my Uncle Buck wanted to make the trip. It was very special having more family there for a difficult situation.

I love you, Johnny. You are a very special man to me and many others.

Chapter 25

REGARDING THE ELDERLY PEOPLE I LOVE:

Think about all that the 100-year-olds have seen in their lifetime, all the knowledge they have obtained. I always show them respect when I see elderly people, I smile at them whenever possible. Just think a minute about a heart beating constantly for 100 years. Amazing to me.

Chapter 26

SOME OF MY FAVORITE SONGS:

More Than A Woman – Bee Gees – I want this played at my funeral.

Suspicious Minds – Elvis Presley

The First Time Ever I Saw Your Face – Roberta Flack

Get Outta My Dreams, Get Into My Car – Billy Ocean

Sleeping With A Friend – Neon Trees

Runaway Train – Soul Asylum

Holiday – Madonna

I Will Always Love You – Whitney Houston

When I Looked At Him – Expose

Could I Have This Dance – Ann Murray

It's Gonna Take A Lot of Love. Nicolette Larson

Wind Beneath My Wings – Bette Midler

Anything by the Bee Gees

Anything by Ricky Martin

Am I Wrong – Nico and Vinz

Best Day Of My Life – American Authors

It's Time – Imagine Dragons

Timber - Pitbull

Classic - MKTO

Rude - Magic

Chandelier - Sia

Believer – American Authors

Shake It Off – Taylor Swift

Chapter 27

I WANTED TO LEAVE THIS EARTH

In 1986 my mom was diagnosed with lung cancer. I was promoted to supervisor in a medical records department at a hospital. I lost all confidence in myself, had low self esteem. I thought to myself I cannot supervise people. I never learned how to do this. I lost a tremendous amount of weight. I wasn't sleeping well. I would wake up in the morning and feel like I only slept one minute every night. My mind was racing. I was crying every day. I gave up all hope. I was very paranoid. My mom and dad tried to talk to me but I wouldn't listen to anything they said.

I attempted suicide. I went to the bathroom and in those days, men had razor blades that came out of the shaver. I took the razor blade out and cut my wrists and neck. They weren't deep cuts. When that didn't work, I filled up the tub and with all my clothes on I laid face down in the tub. But thank God I couldn't do that either. I got out of the tub and ran to my mom who was in her bedroom. I showed her my wrists crying and she screamed – What did you do? She tried to call for help on a landline phone that had a cord on it. I took the cord out of the phone so she couldn't call. Finally I let her take me to the hospital. I still had my wet clothes on when she took me.

I was hospitalized three times for depression. The first hospitalization lasted six weeks. I was very sick.

During the last hospitalization I was laying on my bed in the psych ward. A social worker came in to talk to me. My psychiatrist's name had the word "MAN" in it. I guess I was subconsciously thinking about that man in the garage. My story finally came out to her when I was 28 years old. I am glad it did because then the health professionals were able to treat me so that I could get better. And I did.

During my last hospitalization for depression, I made a plaque made of ceramic with flowers on it and it sits in a wooden frame. Whenever I feel that things are wearing on me, I look at it and say to myself – There is nothing that can happen to me from now on that I would want to harm myself ever again. Nothing anybody says or does to me. I will be strong.

Please don't give up hope. If you are experiencing pain, talk to someone and get help. Talk to someone you trust. It could save your life. If they can't help you, they will find someone who will. I think my mom sent me Dave in 1989. I know that if I didn't meet him then I would have attempted suicide again. He has literally saved my life many times. Please get help if you need it.

Chapter 28

AND NOW SOME STORIES FROM LORI

These stories are not in any chronological order. I went from my notes and as I thought of something I typed it up here.

I love all animals. I hate to see them neglected and abused. When I watch a commercial for the ASPCA I cry instantly. We have to change the channel until its over. I think that people who neglect and abuse pets should have to go the electric chair. You are hurting an innocent animal. Both Sweetie and Sullivan were abused and neglected.

I help save dogs. When I was walking outside regularly in the neighborhood I would be see pooches. There is Snoopy to the right of us, cute as a button. He's a beagle. There is Ginger to the left of us. Ginger likes to bark but that's okay. There is Honey across the street. Too cute. Then there's Lola up the street. I walked past where she was out in her yard. All of a sudden I turned around and Lola had gotten off her leash and was running down the street towards me in the middle of the street. I don't like picking up other people's dogs because I'm afraid I will drop them and hurt them. So I kind of pinned her down gently and waited until her owner came to us. I lifted my hand slightly and she wiggled her way loose. Thankfully she ran into another neighbor's yard where her owner got her. Then there's the boxer down the street. Don't know his name. I again was walking down the street where his owner was trying to get a leash on him. The dog was in the yard. There was a mailman right in front of the house and the man asked him, can you help me catch my dog? The mailman said no. Excuse me, mailmen and dogs. If I was a mailman I wouldn't do it. As I walked closer the man asked, can you help me catch my dog? I said sure. I said come here pooch. He came right to me and the man put the leash on the dog.

I could never be a veterinarian for only one reason. If I had to put an animal to sleep I would cry for 2 days.

There are a lot of people who regularly walk their dogs on our street. I was thinking one day I'm going to set up a newsletter with all the cats and dogs in the neighborhood asking people to submit pictures and stories about their pets. That's on the back burner for now.

I guess dogs just like me. No matter how old they are I call them pup. I talk to them kindly and they respond to me. There was one dog. Little white dog. I have only seen her once. I again was walking and saw her coming towards me from the other side of the street. I always say "hi pooch" to dogs as they pass me by. She came running towards me to where I was standing. She smiled as I was petting her.

Then there's Molly, a brown lab, down the street. She is so beautiful. She has these caramel colored eyes. Her owner said she was about 15 years old. You look into her eyes and she smiles at you and your heart melts. I say hi Molly aren't you a sweetheart and she smiles at me. I then come in the house and cry. Even if I don't get out fast enough to see her, I sit at the kitchen table as she walks by and cry. I don't know what this dog does to me but she is very special.

My dad hated dogs, hated them. He said the only way he would have a dog is if it pooped silver dollars. LOL. We had a dog named Susie. My brother, Bob, was in kindergarten and the teacher said she had a puppy to give away. Would anyone take her? I guess my brother talked to my dad and my brother brought Susie home. She was a collie, a very calm dog. One night I was in my bedroom scared about something. She never came upstairs. I looked out and saw her sitting by my bedroom door watching me. She sat there all night. I guess dogs have a keen sense for their owners. I finally "hounded" my dad to get another dog and he finally said yes. We got Freddy. He was part poodle and Pekinese. He was a small dog and black all over. He was very mean to everyone but me. We named him Freddy because he had a little bit of white hair on his chin. My brother, Bob, in college had a roommate and his name was Freddy and he had a goatee. There, a name was born. We kept him in mostly the kitchen and we had a small gate so he couldn't get into the other parts of the house. When I came home from school my mom would say, Lori's coming up the steps. He would run to the cellar steps and greet me everyday barking with his tail wagging. When my dad would come up the cellar steps, Freddy walked away from the door. There goes that sense again that dogs have. Sadly Freddy lost a fight with a dump truck and was killed. I cried for 3 days. My brother buried him in the backyard.

One summer day my dad asked me to cut the grass. I said I never did it before. He said to cut the grass. I was cutting it and there was a small wall behind me that I didn't see. I slipped and my foot went into the blades. I was very fortunate that I didn't lose my whole foot. My dad drove me to the emergency room. I went inside crying saying that I cut my foot. The nurse took off my shoe and sock and my half of my big toe fell out. Gross! They called in an orthopedic surgeon and took me to surgery to close the wound. I had to spend 3 days in the hospital for antibiotics. I remember an aide came in and saw my foot wrapped up and asked if it was for a bunion. I said no I cut off half my toe. When my mom and dad came to be me in the hospital, I could see how guilty my dad felt. I tried to make him feel better and he did.

I had my gallbladder removed. I kept having attacks the day after Easter and ending up in the emergency room. It happened two years in a row. Doctors figured out it was the kielbasa I ate for Easter Dinner. The second time I had the attack it felt like I was having a heart attack and was up all night. I went to Walt who was visiting and told him and he took me to the emergency room. I'm glad he was there to take me as it was about 3 a.m. I went to a general surgeon and at first I didn't want to have the surgery. He said he could do it laparoscopically then but if it ruptured he would have to cut my abdomen open. I called the next day to schedule the laparoscopic surgery. The hospital didn't have any adult rooms so they put me on the Pediatric floor. On the wall were paintings of Mickey Mouse, Pluto and don't forget Minnie. I took medicine at night and asked the nurse if I could take them. She said she would have to check with the pharmacist. She came back into the room and as if talking to a little kid she said I just talked to Dave, the pharmacist, and he said it was okay to take the medicine. I guess when you are used to talking to little kids all day. The doctor came to see me the next day and examined me. Walt came in a little later that day and I said to him, the doctor saw my private parts. He said a lovely private part it must be. LOL LOL. When I came home from the hospital Dave came over to take care of me. He took me on little walks and made me laugh…again. He was very sweet.

I love elderly people. The older the better. I think that was because when I was little my mom would go visit her lady friends who were probably in their late 60's or 70's. I would always get either pop or chocolate milk and potato chips. I sat there while they gabbed away. I love people in their 90s and especially if they are 100+ years old. Can you imagine a heart beating for over 100 years...constantly? And what about all they have seen in their lives. Medicine, even medications that weren't available to them when they were young, technology, things like TV, elevators, computers, cars, cell phones, microwaves, president assassination, wars, lived through the Depression, man walking on the moon and it goes on.

I won't eat tomatoes. I remember I didn't like them when I was little either. One day my mom was on the telephone. I said I'm going to try a tomato. Took one out of the refrigerator, took a bite and YUK, I still hated them. I can eat chili and spaghetti sauce but won't eat a tomato. I think I could eat it if it was on a hoagie because there are different flavors in there. Weird I know. I was like that when I was young with black olives. Hated them. Now I can eat a whole can of them at one time.

I love baseball and football players when they wear gray uniforms. For some reason their dupa (their butt in Polish) looks really sexy. I always say when I'm watching a game, "nice dupa." Dave says "quit watching the dupas."

Loved Saturday Night Fever, love Disco and love the song "More than a Woman" by the Bee Gees. A beautiful song and a wonderful group. Whenever I would happen to fall asleep when the movie was on and at the end when that song came on I would instantly wake up.

The song "The first time ever I saw your face" by Roberta Flack reminds me of Dave. I always said I would have that song played at my wedding. Not in the church, at the reception because of the last part. Listen to the end and you will see why.

At every baseball home opener, the home team should win. That should be the rule because the home town wants to see a winner the first day.

A total dilemma for a transcriptionist – itching all over the body. This happened to me. When I was working, type a few letters, scratch, type a few letters scratch a different spot, etc.

I remember when cigarettes were sixty-nine cents a pack.

At my first job, I was pure. Madonna's song "Like a Virgin" was popular and I got totally teased about it.

I love military funerals. My dad had one and Dave's dad and uncle had one. When they take the flag off the casket and wrap it in a triangle and give it to a family member, my heart cries. When the soldier brings the flag, he says something that I won't mention here in case someone you love is having a military funeral. My mouth dropped open and Dave's too.

The first movie Dave and I saw was "When Harry Met Sally" - We had to sit in the first row and stretch our necks back so we could see the screen. Too funny. That was when Dave first held my hand. Too sweet.

My catholic grade school was having a Halloween party and we all gathered on the playground for a parade in the neighborhood. I wanted to go as a nun. I drove my mom crazy getting the costume just right. I had black shoes, pantyhose, black skirt, black sweater, holy medal and a black veil that had a strip of white in the front. The nuns were taking pictures of me with other nuns and called the priest over saying look how nice Lori looks.

The word "awesome" is annoying to me. When did they start using it. Also who started using the word "research." Shoot me an e-mail. Who started that phrase??

I hate loud sounds like if someone drops a pot or anything loud on the floor. Walt would always say when I or someone dropped something, Lori doesn't like loud sounds. When they did the gun salute at my dad's funeral, the guy warned us it would be loud. I jumped and said, what the hell was that.

I was daddy's little girl and always will be. He made me feel like a princess.

When I was in grade school learning how to write, I always put the pencil in my left hand and the nuns would put it in my right hand. I told my mom. She called the principal and said don't you make her change hands when she writes. Never had a problem after that. Thanks Mom.

Our priest was in the hospital and the teacher in grade school asked us to each make a card for him. Mine was – on the front it said Get Well Soon. On the inside it said "and that is a Holy Order." Ask a catholic what that means.

Don't be ignorant to me on the phone. If I ever owned a business and got a complaint that you were ignorant, you would be out the door. Also, if I don't know you personally, I will bitch you out on the phone if you are ignorant to me.

I always worry about animals that are outside in the winter. Will they find food and shelter and will they be warm in 3 degree weather.

I have an SUV and it is 12 years old. Nothing wrong with it. No rust and it has been outside for 10 years in the snow and rain. It has only 24,000 miles on it. I never have to have the emissions tested because I drive so few miles a year. Walt's car was nicknamed Cream Puff. He treated it like a baby.

I hate to get tickled. When someone does it I get real mean, combative and yell QUIT IT!

Anything like placemats, pictures on the wall, if a tablecloth is bunched up I have to fix them. Everything has to be symmetric in my eye. If books or papers are crooked I have to fix them.

When Dave and I first got together I found this book that had if you were a Virgo woman and he was an Aries male, would you be compatible. It said we should run away from each other. We are like fire and ice. Proved you wrong 25 years later!

I loved the TV show – Family Affair. Loved Uncle Bill, Buffy, Jody, Sissy, Mrs. Beasley and Mr. French the butler.

Remember the show "Zoom" on PBS? I learned a new language on there. It is called ubbi dubbi. You put an ub before every vowel in the word. My name would be L-UB-OR-UB-I. Say that 10 times fast.

I was maybe 4 or 5 years old. All the cars at that time had seats that went straight across and didn't have a gear shift in the middle. It was on the steering column. I remember standing up in the middle of the seat while my dad drove. You better not do that today. Also, I didn't have a seat belt on.

Walt, my dad, my mom and I were playing Scrabble one time. I used all seven letters spelling the word parfait. I amazed myself. Walt told everybody he knew.

When I was little, one Christmas our whole family went up to my grandmother's house for dinner. I was maybe 6 years old. I think Walt snuck out and he went home to our house and brought out all the wrapped presents and put them under the tree. Then he lit the tree. There was a life size doll there and it was as tall as me. She had a pretty pink dress on and her hair was blonde. I will never forget that.

When electronic things don't work right I get very mad and would like to throw them out the window.

I love the movie Mr. Holland's Opus. At the end when he walks in the auditorium and the whole audience claps for him I cry every time.

Walt and I went to San Diego once. It is beautiful and we both fell in love with that city. It's 72 degrees every day. There was one woman who lived there said, wow, we are having 10% humidity today. Try 110% humidity in Pittsburgh.

Longest word on the left handed side of the keyboard is stewardesses. I think on the right is Monopoly.

When I first started at the doctor's office, the doctor dictated the patient was not able to void. I thought that was something a cashier did at a register when she put in the thing you were buying was somehow wrong. She had to void it out. It means to urinate.

You want a true reality show? Put 10 transcriptionists in an office to work and put a few cameras in there. Now that will be real drama everyday.

When I worked at the doctor's office, back in the old days we called each patient and reminded them of their appointment for the next day. If they didn't answer we left a message saying something like Mr. Smith, this the doctor's office to remind you about your appointment tomorrow at 11 a.m. with Dr. So and So. The next day one of the patients I called was standing at the front desk to make his next appointment. He asked who called me yesterday and left a message on my machine? I said I did (timidly). He just said Very Nice! I didn't if he was talking about my sexy voice or reminding him about the appointment???

The first names of babies are so creative now. And sometimes the spelling is not the norm. I could probably think of about 6 ways to spell Katelyn. It's hard sometimes when you have to bring a patient up on the screen so you can type the report. The MT needs to be creative in thinking of other ways to spell the names. We can usually figure it out.

I think I would be good at coming up with TV commercials because of the creativity in my head.

I was about 7 or so. There was a show on TV and the host was dressed like a captain of a ship and his name was Captain Pitt. His boat was called the Nancy B. He said to send in a rhyme and he will read it on the air. I sent one in saying that I made up:

> Sailing, sailing on the Nancy B.
> My name is Lori and I'll tell you a story on the Nancy B.

I was home sick one day and he read my poem. I was so excited.

Transcriptionists were multi-taskers way before the word came popular.

I remember watching the Elvis concert that he did in Hawaii in 1973. I sat in my mom and dad's bedroom and watched it. I fell in love with him while he did the concert. I still love him today. At our bowling league, they had Karaoke night. There was a guy who did Suspicious Minds by Elvis. He sounded exactly like Elvis, it was eerie.

I never poop on Saturday. Not sure why.

Dave and I went to see Sam Kinnison. He did this thing where he asked the audience if any man had his heart broken by a woman. A man raised his hand. Kinnison asked him what was the girlfriend's name.

He gave Kinnison the girl's phone number and Kinnison called her. She answered and let's just say he let her have it yelling kind of loud and asking her why she broke this guy's heart. He went on for a couple minutes. I am totally serious. I laughed so hard I couldn't breathe in or let air out of my lungs. I thought I was going to pass out for a second, I was scared. But it was worth it. My biggest laugh ever.

When someone says "czekaj" to you, it just means wait in Polish. It's pronounced "check eye". We have always said that check eye was a Polish eye doctor. Think about it.

The boss I have now wasn't the boss when she said this to me. She was trying to teach me something and I didn't quite understand and I said I was Polish. She said, oh that explains a lot. Now I know how to teach you things.

I was probably in about the 4th grade. Our teacher said to write a single sentence about something in the news. I went home and found out that President Nixon had pneumonia. I write down the sentence. The next day I go to school. The teacher said, Lori it's your turn. I said PRESIDENT NIXON HAS AMMONIA. I was very proud until the teacher yelled it's PNEU-monia. I sat down and shut up.

I took Tap and Baton classes when I was young. I went every Saturday. We were in a parade once. We were all dressed up and started walking down the street doing our routine. I happened to glance in the crowd and mom and dad on the sidewalk. My mom waved. They were so proud of me. I think that's were I got my rhythm and love to dance.

I can't be late for doctor's appointments or any appointment that comes up. I would rather be an hour early and sit there rather than being 2 minutes late. Walt was the same way.

Dave and I went to Las Vegas once and he ate some bad sausage at breakfast. He was throwing up in the bathroom. I cannot take anyone I love who is sick and vomiting. I held a pillow over my ears until he was done. I went to give him a kiss and he said – I have puke breath. I said that's okay and gave him a tender kiss on the cheek. Now that's love!

The best present I ever got from Walt was 500 pens with my little transcription company's name and my phone number. He bought those so I could hand them out to people and maybe get some more business. He always thought of the most clever presents.

If there is a smudge on something made of glass I have to clean it off. Walt and my Aunt Annie were the same way.

I said when I got married for the dance with my dad I would want – The Wind Beneath My Wings by Bette Midler. Listen to the words really close and you'll see why I wanted this song.

I think Disco music opened the flood gates for future music and lyrics. It really started something. K.C. and the Sunshine Band, Bee Gees, Gloria Gaynor and Donna Summer just to name a few.

In my little business I typed for a very prominent doctor. I have a note that she sent me thanking me for typing her dictations so well. I have it framed on my desk and will treasure it always.

I remember when I heard my mother said the F-word for the first time. I cried. My mom doesn't swear!

I went to a Community College for medical records technology. I didn't want to go a 4 year college because I felt my mom and dad didn't have the money to send me to one. I wanted to be a second grade math teacher. So one day I got a catalog from my school and decided on what I would study and decided on Medical Record Technology.

I worked for my aunt in her small restaurant when I was about 16. There was an older man that came in every Saturday and he was always looped. He would only come in for coffee. He always gave me 3 or 4 dollar tips. For a coffee. My aunt whispered to me one take him his coffee, he'll give you a good tip. He always did.

I love the stores where you can buy stuff for a dollar. You can have fun just with 5 or 10 bucks and look at all you get. Walt would have had a field day with those kind of stores.

Soap operas don't use landline phones anymore. They whip out their cell phones and say I have to take this and walk away from whomever they were talking to. When did that start?

Our parents drank a lot in the 50's and 60's. And then they drove home from the party or club where they were dancing. I don't know how they made it home sometimes. They must have had their Guardian angle looking over them…..thank goodness.

Ask a non-Virgo what time it is, they'll they say about 20 minutes after 9. Ask a Virgo and they will say its 9:16. We have to be precise.

As I said before I love the movie Saturday Night Fever. Whoever taught John Travolta to dance must have been brilliant. John has been dancing ever since and very well I might add.

My brother, dad, Dave and I went to a great seafood restaurant in our area. We ordered whole lobsters. I didn't know you had to crack it all apart to eat it. I said I can't do it. The waitress came over and I asked her to do it. She said we really aren't allowed to touch peoples' food. I said it was okay so she cracked it open a little to get it started. I said after I CAN'T DO IT, I CAN'T DO IT. I then ordered a shrimp dinner instead.

One time one of my fellow students in grade school was bad in class. The teacher told me to take him to the principal's office which I did. We get there and she asks the boy what he did he told her. She looked at me and said what did you do? I said I didn't do anything, Sister, I just brought him here.

How stoned were the writers of the show Gilligan's Island. All those people who came to the island and the stranded folks still couldn't get rescued. I would yell at the TV – Skipper, the man with the big plane is right behind you. Turn around!. He never turned around. Or, Gilligan, the man with the big boat is to your left. Behind the palm tree. Turn left. For God's sake look left! He never looked left. I watched it every week hoping maybe they would be rescued that week. But how did Mr. and Mrs. Howell have different outfits all the time. How many suitcases do you pack for only a three hour tour, a three hour tour? They never got sunburned. Their batteries never ran out. The women's hair was always fixed perfectly and they had perfect makeup. The men were always clean shaven. How many razors do you take on a three hour tour? A three hour tour. And the Skipper. He weighed let's say about 260. After 4 years on the island he still weighed 260. What did they eat on the island? A lot of fruit, maybe fish. I'm not sure if they killed any animals to cook on the island. He's on the Mediterranean Diet! How could he still weigh 260 after four years on the diet (the show was on from September, 1964 to September, 1967 – 98 episodes). Let's talk poop for just a minute. Seven people on the island. Seven poops a day, assuming they were all regular. With all the fruit, that's a good assumption. Forty-nine poops a week x 52 weeks is 2,548 poops a year x 4 years is 10,192 poops. There's not enough sand in the world to cover all that poop. And let's say they did bury it. Did they put a stick or rock to indicate where the poop was buried? So that when they did another burial, they didn't accidently dig up a previous poop burial. I read online that the island was estimated to be about 200-400 square miles. That's still not enough sand to cover all that poop. But then again, maybe the writers weren't stoned. We tuned in every week and watched every rerun. Keep hope alive, right! Eventually they did get rescued because I remember there was a big parade for them when they came home.

One Saturday Dave came over and we both fell asleep. I was on the couch and he was on the recliner. The buzzer rang and we both jolted up. I said here take the phone???? He said okay. He went down to the door and it was a pizza delivery guy who had the wrong apartment. Why did

I hand him the phone and why did we say okay???? We always laugh about this one.

My keyboard has the letters on it almost all rubbed off. Why don't I get another one? This one is just getting broken in.

When you are looking for something you can't find, say this prayer aloud. You will find it pretty fast. A girl at my one job taught me this:

> Dear St. Anthony, come around,
> Something lost, and can't be found.

It always works. If you don't find it in a day or two it probably was thrown away.

I love when people pick their noses in a car. Helloooooo, there are only six windows around you, we can see what you are doing.

On every and all females, I have to check out their purse to see if it is nice or not.

Kids learn computers now in the first or second grade. I didn't see a computer until I was 19.

I was about 17. It was snowing and my mom wanted to go check out the new mall in our area. I said okay. I really didn't know the area then. I took a wrong turn and ended up on a snow covered road and it was a pretty steep hill. I started sliding and I panicked and I yelled MA! We landed a little bit a guy's hard. My mom went up to the door and asked for help. The nice gentleman came down and backed up the car so it was now on the road. That nice man must have let my mom use the phone (no cell phones in that day)

and my Dad and brother came and drove us home. I am so scared to drive in the snow. Always have since that time. I really hate ice on streets. I take Dave to the bus stop and in the winter I say, what's the temperature? He will say 38 degrees. I say that's only 6 degrees above freezing!!!!

Like Sheldon on Big Bang Theory, I too am sarcasm illiterate.

Did you notice that today there are no female babies named Lori, Linda or Susan.

I loved the old show Medical Center. Chad Everett was totally hot!. Dr. Joe Gannon, thoracic surgeon. I watched him every week and drooled a little, okay a lot. I think that he is why I got into the health field.

When I was taking shorthand in high school, I would practice on my thumb making the words while I watched TV. I did that for many years but I don't do it so much now. I was the best shorthand student but maybe not. The teacher would say a paragraph and we would write it down in shorthand. I got up to 120 words which is pretty good. After the dictation I looked at the teacher, she asked did you get it? I said I think so. I did.

About my accounting teacher in high school. The business section had the four classrooms around a supply room. He was yelling at someone and told him to go into the supply room. A lot of yelling and hitting what I thought was cabinets. We were horrified. The teacher and student came out. We found out later that he told the student to pretend like I'm hitting you and the teacher hit the metal cabinets with his hand. He didn't hurt the student at all. That teacher also taught me something. It's better to have it and not need it than to need it and not have it. After that I always had an umbrella in my bag for years and years. What if it rains and I don't have an umbrella?

A question for you. The house is on fire. All people and pets are safe outside. What is the one thing you would grab out of that house? I would take my mom and dad's wedding pictures. Everything can be replaced but them.

One time while Dave was cleaning off the car in the winter, he scraped off the little nozzle where the windshield washer fluid comes out. I went to a dealer to have it fixed. I then went to the grocery store to get a couple things. When we got home, Dave told me I had two different shoes on. I had on a gray/white tennis shoe on my left foot and a purple/white tennis shoe on my right foot. What???

I want to thank my cousin, Joyce, for something she did to raise my self esteem. On my birthday two years ago we went for a spa day. We got our hair done, went to a wonderful Chinese restaurant for lunch and then went to a beauty store to have a makeup makeover. Joyce told the woman at the beauty place to do whatever she (me) wants to make her feel good about herself. Well, it worked. I now put on makeup every day and fix my hair just right when before I would just slap on some foundation. Thank you, Joyce, for doing that for me. I will never forget it.

Chapter 29

MY FETISHES:

- Purses – I was never a shoe person. I don't think I have a pair of dress shoes.
- Bags.
- Wallets.
- Books – I once went back and back to buy bibles. I didn't like the one I bought so I kept buying. I bought about 10-12 of them in a short period of time. I never thought to return the ones I bought previously. Just kept buying.
- CD's.
- DVD's.
- Cell Phones.
- Pens – it has to have a cap on it. If it doesn't have one and is supposed to, I throw it away, never to be used again. Even if it's new.
- Fitness and exercise books.
- Online shopping.
- Looking for books for my E-reader. You can get books for 99 cents!
- Calculators – They have to have rubber keys and have a good look to the numbers when they come up on the little screen.
- Pittsburgh Pirates T-shirts.
- Dogs and puppies.
- Office supplies, pens, sticky notes, whatever. I love it in summer right before school starts. All the supplies are right there in the stores.
- Polar Bears – They are losing their homes due to global warming.

SOME MORE STORIES: When I was in high school they asked if any of us would like to work in the business office during the summer. I said I would. I had to fill out an application. The question read - Why do you want this position? I didn't say for the experience, or learn the machines in the office. I wrote, so I could buy things. C'mon. I was only 16…and honest.

I never had a period of my own. The doctor I have now put me on hormones for many years so I would have a period. I said one day – I don't need a period to tell me I'm a girl and he took me off the medication, but still gave me the hormones at a lower dose so it wouldn't bring on a period.

I was supervisor in a Medical Records Dept for about 5 minutes when the boss asked me to call on some subpoenas to see if they were pending or were resolved. I called the first one. Is Ada Brown there? Girl on the phone said do you mean ADA Brown. I said yes, is she there?. She gave me the information. I called the second one and this one was also named Ada. Weird but okay. I asked if Ada Green was there. She said do you mean Assistant District Attorney Green. I realized what ADA stood for and was totally embarrassed. Walt had a field day telling his courthouse buddies at work. Hilarious. C'mon in my own defense there are women named Ada in the world!!

There was a Pittsburgh Pirate by the name of Tim Foli #10 in the 1970s. I really liked him. I made a huge sign that said "We heart sign Foli. I was so excited. I get to the stadium and I put the sign up. All of a sudden, Tim Foli is on the field and he is looking up towards my way. Then he waves and tips his cap. WOW. I told everybody what he did. Totally cool!

I tell people who ask what I do for a living and they say oh, you are a typist. I want to put a firecracker in my nose, light it, open my eyes and watch my head explode! Not that typists aren't wonderful mind you.

It was kind of hard learning to write my last name, I had to write 9 letters.

Why do baseball batters get struck out, on the way back to the dugout they take a few looks at the pitcher thinking you think you are so tough, I'll get you next time?

Chapter 30

THE BIG "B"

My first job began on May 18, 1981 and I was 19 years old. I turned 20 in September. From the first day I started spending money. I got many, many credit cards. If a company would send me an application for a credit card I would fill it out and mail it back. About a week later the card came in the mail. I would go shopping every Sunday with my Aunt Annie. We went everywhere. I would come home with 4-5 bags every week. If I saw I purse that cost $800.00 I would buy it. Then I thought well I have to have the wallet and bag to match. I didn't worry about the bills. I would send the minimum payment every month, maybe a little more. I had about 15 credit cards.

When I went part time from my full time job, I was writing out bills one day. This was in 2010. I always write down the place and the amount of the payment I would send each month on a piece of paper to see who I had to pay and how much. It was when credit card companies were getting bold and wanted at least $100.00 per month. I didn't have the money. I started to panic. Finally I called my lawyer and said I think we need to do the "B" word. Bankruptcy. I was $53,000.00 in debt. My lawyer said to not make any more payments and for the companies to call him if they had any questions. The phone was ringing off the hook all day every day. I had to go to Bankruptcy court. This was after I hit my head off the door and I was very fuzzy. I met my lawyer at his office and we walked to the bus stop which was maybe a quarter of a mile away. Also at this point I injured my left shin and had to use a cane to get around. I go to the court and had to answer some questions about my situation. It wasn't long after that that I was approved for the bankruptcy (04/12/2011). I was afraid they would repossess my car but that didn't happen, thank goodness.

My advice to anyone who wants to spend money foolishly. DON'T DO II!! Save your money. When I was at my first job in a hospital my dad would say save your money, you are going to need it some day. My mother always told him it was my money and I could spend it any way I wanted. I wish I had listened to my dad. I am slowly building up my credit again and not being foolish about it. I have no money in the savings account and wish I had saved that money. I think I got the bug for spending when I was about 16. This was back in about 1977. I made a whopping $1.25 an hour and tips on the weekends. I always had money. I bought my own clothes and school lunches. In fact one time I was in gym class and I had a small change purse full of tips that I put in a locker without a lock. Someone stole it.

Again, SAVE YOUR MONEY!! It isn't worth having 20 or 30 expensive purses when one will do the job. Dave once said to me he has one wallet with money in it and I have 10 wallets with no money in it. He was right.

Chapter 31

MY HEROES THAT I ADMIRE

I had a wonderful teacher in grade school. I'll never forget her, Mrs. C. I went to a catholic school but they did have lay teachers meaning they weren't nuns. She was the coolest teacher. She would tell us stories about her husband. I wanted to be a teacher just like her when I grew up. I wanted to be an elementary math teacher. I had a chalkboard in the basement and I would pretend I was teaching my imaginary students math. There was this cool little store near us that sold books but in the bunch there were a few that were teacher books meaning they had the answers in them. I found an elementary math book. I was in heaven. I found a couple other teacher books but the math book was my favorite.

One day, another girl in our class in grade threw up at her desk and it went everywhere. One day she was absent and someone had to use her desk and didn't want to because it was vomited on. Mrs. C said if a person in your house threw up in the toilet in the bathroom you still use it don't you? She had a point. That's how cool she was. She would write out her bills while we were doing stuff in class.

My other hero is a doctor who lived next to us at home. Her name is Joanne. I admire her the most of all. She is a very intelligent woman. She was an endocrinologist and very well known in her profession and retired a couple of years ago. She was the first woman President of the Medical Staff at her hospital. She was also the first woman Vice-President of Medical Affairs. Anyhow, one day my brother was in his room and had a problem with his private parts and his zipper. My mom's trying to figure out how to handle this. She went next door and asked Joanne to help. I'm not sure how but she got it done but she did. When Joanne went to medical school in the 60's there were only a few women there studying to be doctors. When my dad died, she came down to the funeral home to see him. I looked at the woman kneeling and saying a prayer for my dad and I finally recognized it was Joanne. She came to me and hugged me. I was ready to cry but held it together. I admire this woman like no one else. She is very special to me.

Chapter 32

MY INJURIES

In 2011 one day I was in our second bedroom with a round basket of laundry in my hands and that is our messy room with a lot of things on the floor. I started to fall and instead of bracing myself so I wouldn't hit the door, I held on to the stupid basket. Smacked my head against a door. I really don't know if it knocked me out for a little bit or not. I got up and there was a big bump on my head. It took a good 2-1/2 to 3 years for me to be back to normal, my normal. I injured my shin around the same time, I must have torn something really bad because the pain was so unbearable. I would hobble to the car to take Dave to the bus stop and screaming and crying. He asked me what's the matter. I cried that my shin hurts. It was numb for about 2 years and a small part of it is still numb. I went to the hospital ER and had a CT scan of my head for the head injury. It came back normal, but I was very fuzzy for a couple of years. Sometimes I would forget the last word to a sentence I am saying. Also, sometimes I could describe a person but I can't think of their name. I had shaking in my left hand and a little less in my right when I hold something. I recently went to a neurologist for the shaking. He said it is nothing to worry about. I asked if it was the beginning of Parkinson's disease and he said no, it was probably from the head trauma.

Chapter 33

THE GARAGE

I don't remember how old I was, I think I have blocked it out of my brain. I might have been about 9. There were three girls and I just hanging out on the sidewalk talking. An adult male neighbor came out and said – Let's play hide and go seek. We said okay. He took me to another neighbor's garage to "hide." We get in there and he pulls me to his side and puts him arm around me. He then undoes his zipper and brings out his penis. He tried to make me hold it. He got my four fingers around it but when he tried to put my thumb around it, I tried so hard to not let him do it. Something told me to not let him bend my thumb. I straightened my thumb with all my might so he couldn't bend it. This is maybe a 30-year-old man and I am 9. He couldn't do it. Finally he let me go and I ran home. I remember running from the garage and it was a sunny day but once I reached my yard, everything is a blank to me. For many years I would think about that person every day and what he did. That is probably why I didn't have a boyfriend until I was 28 years old. I was too scared. The only men I trusted were my dad and brothers.

When I was hospitalized the third time for depression, a social worker came to see me. I started crying hysterically and I told her the story. My psychiatrist's name has "MAN" in his last name. I think it kept bringing me back to that day in the garage. After that day, I could see from my school pictures that I was getting heavier and heavier. I was trying to dull the pain mostly with potato chips.

I told Dave about it one day. Ever since then I don't think about that man because I have my honey to think about instead.

I would always say as I got older that I hoped that man didn't do that to other little girls. Maybe someone called the police on him I always hoped.

I often wondered when I was older, what if he was able to bend my thumb. What other terrible things would he have done to me? I think my Guardian Angel was with me that day protecting me. Everyone has a Guardian Angel. Pray to him or her every day and that Angel will protect you.

Chapter 34

THEY DESERVE A CHAPTER OF THEIR OWN:

They are the six most gorgeous men in the universe.

1) My Dave Herzig. Hot! He is the most beautiful man in my world.

2) Ricky Martin – Beautiful man and father. He sings a song and has a video called "The Best Thing About Me Is You." This song changed my life for the better. If you listen to the words he is singing and watch the video I am sure you will agree. In the song he sings "I think I'm cool cause your name's on this heart-shaped tattoo." I got a tattoo with Ricky in one heart and Dave in another heart. The tattoo artist put banners around it and a couple of purple flowers. Thank you, Ricky, for changing my life.

3) Garrett Jones – Baseball player who sadly left the Pittsburgh Pirates. A very sad day in my life. Beautiful eyes.

4) Joe Manganiello – Had to have him in this book. He's a Pittsburgh boy! Very hot!!! Dave says he has a bromance going with Joe. LOL.

5) Dr. Travis Stork. ER physician and cohost on a medical information show. Beautiful man. Love his smile.

6) Billy Gardell. Star of a TV show. Not only is he also a Pittsburgh boy but he is a total Pittsburgh Steelers fan like Joe. Wave that Terrible Towel proud, Billy!! Totally adorable. He has a beautiful smile, too.

Chapter 35

PITTSBURGHESE – OUR OWN LANGUAGE

I finally figured it out living in Pittsburgh. We have our own language here. Now, I don't mean to insult Pittsburghers. That is not my intention. I have Pittsburgh Pride. I have just made a few observations during my over 50 years in the Burgh.

Pittsburghers can't pronounce words that have OU in them, an example is house, it comes out as haas.

We can't say words that have the letters OW in them. Downtown comes out as dahntahn.

We can't say words that end in ING, I'm goin to the store.

We also can't pronounce words that begin with TH. Ex: Is zat right? Are you gonna eat 'at?

It's so funny to watch the Pittsburgh news because they interview someone and you can hear the way we say our words.

Some people say warsh instead of wash. I say woosh.

Some people say yinz. (probably meaning you guys). And there is n'nat. Probably meaning "and that".

Sometimes we don't pronounce the letter T in the middle of words. Center comes out as cenner. Hunter is Hunner. Etc.

We also say fihr (as one syllable) for fire where most people make it two syllables. Same thing with towel. We say tile. Bile for bowel. We say shire for shower. We Pittsburghers are great at making two syllable words into one. We can even make a three syllable word two syllables. An example is probably. We make it probly.

Sometimes we even make four words into two. Jeetyet? Meaning did you eat yet?

Dill, fill, rill, still. These words are actually deal, feel, real and steel. That's how we say them.

We don't say the word "to." We say "ta." I'm going ta school.

I was in a conference call for work with other MT's located all over the country. I must have said something that I think sounded funny to them. After I said my sentence there was about 4 seconds of dead silence and then they said, oh, okay. They had to figure out what I was saying.

When my brother moved to Meadville, they made fun of his Pittsburgh accent. I think he said they tried to teach him how talk correctly. And he did. But when he came home to visit, the accent came right back to him. He said that he heard some people say MUPPEER from Pittsburgh. I asked him what that meant? He said it's people that say I'm up here from Pittsburgh.

We call rubber bands gum bands. Don't know why. We say buggy for shopping cart. Also don't know why.

Chapter 36

I WANT TO KNOW WHO MADE UP THESE NAMES FOR URINATION:

Pee
Pee-Pee
Whiz (my dad always used this one)
Squirt
Leak
Tap a kidney.
Tinkle
Piddle
Trickle
Piss

AND WHO MADE THESE NAMES UP FOR BOWEL MOVEMENTS:

Poop
Turd
Poo Poo
Crap
Easter Bunny's present.
Drop a load of logs in the water.
Drop some friends off at the lake.

Chapter 37

WHAT HATS PEOPLE WEAR WHEN WORKING AT HOME. THESE ARE ALSO WHAT MOMS AND DADS PRACTICALLY DO EVERY DAY.

1) Activities Coordinator
2) Decision Maker
3) Lost and Found Department
4) Budget Coordinator
5) Telephone Operator
6) Appointment Scheduler
7) Book Reader – to the little kids
8) Personnel Director
9) Menu Planner
10) Child Psychology
11) Language Specialist
12) Comedy Relief Specialist
13) Dog Treat Dispenser
14) IT Support Department – Computer Repair
15) Debt Consolidation Expert
16) Timekeeper
17) Birthday Tracker
18) TV Remote Locator
19) Nose Cleaner and/or Wiper
20) Fashion Coordinator
21) Energy Conservationist
22) Pest Control
23) Bathroom Attendant
24) Dispute Resolver
25) Medication Distribution
26) Job Seeker

27) Taxi Driver

28) Information Desk Clerk

29) Secretarial Specialist

30) Musical Coordinator

31) Taste Tester

32) Transportation Director

33) Sign For Packages that are delivered

34) Current Events Coordinator

35) Cheerer-Upper

36) Calmer-Downer

37) Security Officer

38) Accountant

39) Mail Collector and Distribution

40) Health Care Coordinator

41) Detective

42) Cook

43) Maid

44) Fire Prevention Duty

45) Internet Specialist

46) Teacher's Aide

47) Wedding Planner

48) Dog Catcher and Trainer

49) Nutrition and Fitness Expert

50) Pharmacy Assistant

Chapter 38

THE "LOVE YOU" PROGRAM

Before I go to the conclusion of my book I would like to start a program called the "Love You" program.

When you see someone you love, before you leave each other say Love You. Say it to others by phone, text, email, and any of the social medias out there. Say it to your friends. Say it to your family, your husband, your wife, your brothers, your sisters, your sons, your daughters, your aunts, your uncles, your cousins, your grandparents, your grandchildren, your great grandchildren, your boyfriend and girlfriend, anyone you love and are in contact with. You do not know if that will be the last time you see them or talk to them. I mentioned earlier in this book that any one of them can be taken from you in an instant. Look at the tragedy of the people who died in 9/11. Almost 3,000 people went about their usual routine, went to work one day or got on a plane and never came back home. Every day that I drop Dave off at the bus stop in the morning we say we love each other and after he gets out of the car I say please, Lord, bring him back home to me safe.

Case in point. My brother, Walt, died before my dad, my brother Bob, or I got to say goodbye and I love you. Another case in point, Dave came home from work one day to find that his mother died of a heart attack in the family room. He never got to say good bye and I love you one final time. His mom died on Walt's birthday, September 12th. Look at Robin Williams and Joan Rivers who recently died. Their families never got the chance to say I love you and say goodbye to them. Now their families have their tragedies in their lives that they have to deal with every day. I hope and pray that they and others in their families can one day move forward and see a happy life ahead. I always say think of the happy times you had together and it will help you get through your tragedy. Say "Love You." It takes one second to say and has two syllables. At the end of your texts, emails and social medias, if you don't want to write out "love you," just put LY. It will mean the same. I promise it won't hurt.

IN CONCLUSION

As I finish this book I hope I gave you a chuckle or two with my rhymes and the transcription songs and stories that I shared. I mostly smiled as I was writing this book but sad at some other times. I wrote about my personal life to help people that go through tragedies in their life and let them know that they can still be happy no matter what happens to them. I found a man who loves me when I thought nobody would. I realized that my mom, dad and two brothers was/is special to me and they love me and I love them all. As I said earlier I think my brother, Walt, sent me the inspiration from heaven to write this book, like the book he never was able to write. This was for you Walt, I love you. If you are in pain about a tragedy or challenge that has happened to you, please talk to someone. I held in my pain about my being molested as a young child for 19 years before I told anybody. That is too long to be in pain. An hour is too long to hold something like that inside you. Please, please tell someone.

As I said in the introduction of this book, your tragedies are not who you are. You are a good person who had some things happen to you. You can move forward and lead a happy life. I think Walt Whitman said it so beautifully – Keep your face always toward the sunshine and shadows will fall behind you.

Before I go, I cannot end this book without giving a special thank you to my eye doctor, Dr. Antonio Chirumbolo. He suggested I self publish on an e-book and started the proverbial ball rolling and I got my book published in paperback form. You started the positive Karma. Thank you so much! Don't forget. If this book does well, you are getting that gigantic gift I promised you. What's your favorite color?

One other thing, I typed this whole book on my computer. I typed 141,251 characters with spaces. Yikes! No wonder my arthritic, man hands hurt!

Someone once asked a 100+ person how to live a long life. That 100-year-old person said "you never hear of anyone dying of happiness." Be happy!

Oh, One more thing:

Dave and I are getting married July 24, 2015 after being together 25 years. We picked July 24th because that was the day of our Friday Night Summer Bowling League way back in 1989. It was a very good year! That's also the day we got our dog, Sullivan, in 2013. Wish us well!

Take care and love you!

Lori

About the Author

My name is Lori Radosny, and I live in Pittsburgh, PA. I am fifty-three years old. I am currently a medical transcriptionist and working at home for a transcription company out of state. I have been a transcriptionist for over thirty-three years, more than half my life. I started working at a hospital full-time when I was just nineteen years old. I fell in love with medical transcription in 1981, especially radiology, after helping the radiology department where I worked. From then I was hooked. I love transcription because I feel it is an important part of a patient's care. I always strive to transcribe a perfect report. I currently live with my fiancé and our dog, Sullivan. Dave and I are getting married on Friday, July 24, 2015, the same date that we met in our bowling league in 1989.